TEEN ANGST

D0104339

TEEN ANGST

A Celebration
of REALLY
Bad Poetry

EDITED BY **Sara Bynoe**

 **St. Martin's Griffin
New York**

TEEN ANGST. Copyright © 2005 by Sara Bynoe. Foreword copyright © 2005 by Morgan C. McCormack. All rights reserved. Printed in the United States of America. No part of this book may be used or reproduced in any manner whatsoever without written permission except in the case of brief quotations embodied in critical articles or reviews. For information, address St. Martin's Press, 175 Fifth Avenue, New York, N.Y. 10010.

www.stmartins.com

Library of Congress Cataloging-in-Publication Data

Teen angst : a celebration of really bad poetry / edited by Sara Bynoe.—1st ed.
p. cm.
ISBN 0-312-33474-5
EAN 978-0312-33474-1

1. Teenagers' writings, American. 2. Teenagers' writings, Canadian. 3. Teenagers—Poetry. 4. Canadian poetry. 5. American poetry. I. Bynoe, Sara.

PS591.T45 T44
811.008'09283—dc22   2004048906

D 10 9 8 7 6 5 4 3

APR 2 4 2017

Contents

Breakups--"I Will Never Love Again" Poems

More Than Like--Love Poems

I Am Alone--and No One Understands My Pain Poems

Obvious Metaphors—Life Is a Mountain, a Road . . .

School (Poems About Cliques and Math Class)

Life Sucks and I Want to Die Poems

Fuck You--You Don't Understand Me!

Political Action--Fight the Power Poems

Pointless Ramblings--Poems Made Up of Words That the Author Thought Sounded "Good" Together

Odes--To Famous People That Felt Your Pain Like Kurt Cobain

For Fun--Silly Poems About Silly Things

Other--Self-Appointed Themes

Many Thanks to:

My Father and Mother for all their support, encouragement, advice, and love.

My brother David for all his help along the way, with the Web site and his Robot angst; without you this would never have happened.

Craig Robertson for all his time and fabulous work on the Web site.

Sarah Rankin and Joleen Sadler who both stuck by me through all the angst and who know all my secrets.

Erin Millar, Michelle Bjolverud, Kate Nosen, Sasha, Mali Kos, Jeanette Burman, Helen Devine, Emily Robinson, and my Soupy Sister, who have supported my teen angst poetry endeavors from the very beginning.

All my classmates at Mount Royal College and my classmates at Studio 58 especially Lisa Oppenheim, Emily Cain, Kristina Murphy, Nicola Correia-Damude, Joe MacLeod, and Zack Taylor, who supported and indulged me in this idea.

Jane Heyman, Allison Kelly, Aaron Bushkowsky, Sherri Sadler, and Kathryn Shaw for their support, advice, and encouragement in this project.

Sarah Heller and Elizabeth Bewley for seeing the potential in this project and for all their help along the way.

Special thanks to all the people who I loved and hurt me in the end.

The Flava and everyone who caused me angst in my life; without you I'd have nothing to write about.

To everyone that came to a reading or who wanted to come but never actually did—thanks for keeping the dream alive and thanks for your laughs.

A special thanks to the lovely ladies at the Calgary Public Library—because you are so special to me.

Introduction

Hi. My name is Sara, and I . . . I wrote teen angst poetry.

You know what I'm talking about, those poems you wrote and filled journals with when you were a teenager, when you were angsty.

It is a shameful secret that many of us keep from the world. Hiding these secret journals in the closets of our bedrooms in our parents' houses. But, it's time to admit it: I wrote teen angst poetry. You wrote teen angst poetry. We all wrote teen angst poetry.

In the course of my adolescence I spent hours hidden away writing in my bedroom, which I wanted to paint black but, of course, wasn't allowed to so it was a "light pink"—very uncomplementary to the feelings I held inside; the feelings that I only shared with these journals. Five to be exact, filled with poetry written during the years 1990–1998 (not to mention the countless loose pages with poetry that are floating around).

Yes, I wrote *a lot* of teen angst poetry. Yeah, I had a lot of angst. I'm not exactly sure why, perhaps it's my overdramatic nature, but something would spark me almost daily, some overwhelming feeling of sadness or loneliness or pain and these feelings would be intolerable until I wrote a poem. I would seclude myself in my room, light my candles, put on music (The Cranberries, Sarah McLachlan, and Enya were the preferred) and the words would fall out of my pen like water out a faucet. There was never any censoring, hardly any editing, and only one draft; that was the moment—that was my teen angst.

Most of my teen angst poetry stems from my love life; lack there of or frustrations with. I was always either in "more than like," "I will never love again," or "I am alone and no one understands my pain" mode. At the time these feelings were very real and these poems expressed exactly what I wanted to say but couldn't share with the cruel world. But time has passed since I originally felt "more than like" and that "no one understands my pain" and okay, to be honest, not a lot of time has passed since I felt that "I would never love again."

Actually, it was in one of those "I will never love again" moods that I rediscovered my teen angst poetry and came to create www.TeenAngstPoetry.com and consequently this book. I had just been dumped or I hadn't had a boyfriend in a while; I can't remember which since the cycle has repeated itself so many times now. I was chatting with a friend on the phone when I came across a binder (yes, a binder—about one-hundred-plus pages) full of poetry given to me by my high school boyfriend. I read this poetry to her, which was given and received in "love" and laughed at it. Laughed at out loud, with tears rolling down my face. There was one particularly awful line in one poem that went something like "with my peripheral vision I have seen your eyes divert to the path made for one," that made me keel over. It was some obvious metaphor poem about our life paths.

After the tears were wiped away and she had played me the song that her ex wrote for her, "You are the cherry on my ice-cream sunday, I want to love you all ways in one day," I began to feel the creepy and bad feeling of karma. To rectify this I knew I had to share my teen poems with her—and to my amazement my stuff was even worse. Even more startling was that my own poetry made me fall flat in laughter. My friend then got out her old poetry and amidst laughing and gasps for air www.TeenAngst Poetry.com was born.

To celebrate the launch of the Web site in December of 2000, the very first ever Teen Angst Poetry reading was held (at a bar called the Newt—which years later, oddly enough, was turned in to a swank restaurant that one guy I knew (who I wrote some angsty poems about) ended up as head chef at . . . but I digress). It was a small gathering of friends and friends of friends. The only way I can describe what went on that night was it felt like a poetry reading meets stand-up comedy in an AA sort of way. I wish you could have been there; we laughed so hard some literally peed their pants. The readings after that expanded to include performance art and music. For a while we even had a theme song when my friend Jeanette would come out—the song is called "Anthem for the Disrespected" and the chorus goes "Die, Die, Die,/Fuck off and Die./Die, Die, Fuck off, and Die." It is a great tune, in a country/ blues style that I hope she one day records and makes a million from. Another aspect to the readings is the teen angst poetry game. This is where I, the host, read current song lyrics as poems to show everyone that teen angst poetry is all around us—living on and making millions.

See, I wrote teen angst poetry. You wrote teen angst poetry. And Alanis Morrisette wrote teen angst poetry, too.

It's true. You live, you learn—from your past. I have learned a lot since I created www.TeenAngstPoetry.com. Now when I feel angst coming on I know that I have the choice to seclude and feel sorry for myself or I can acknowledge my feelings and realize that I am not alone in my woes and that time will heal.

On the pages that follow I hope that you will relate to the

heartbreaks and anxieties of the authors because teen angst is universal. You may have once been hiding in your room thinking that "no one understood your pain," when in fact your best friend was doing the exact same thing blocks away. I hope you laugh at the awkwardness of rhymes and metaphors, as much as the authors laugh at them now. I hope you give yourself a big pat on the back for surviving teenagedom. As tough as it can be, some good things can be produced in it. And I do understand your pain.

—Sara Bynoe
creator of www.TeenAngstPoetry.com

Foreword

The following is a blurb taken out of Morgan's poetry book. I think it sums up what a lot of teens think about their own poetry and why they write it:

I don't know.

I guess it's easier than a journal, this little spiral-bound notebook full of poems. Yes, it is deeply personal, but not so serious, not so specific. In a poem there is a detached sense of being "a poem writer," not a person with personal problems, and not some lovesick teenager with a major case of infatuation. I get to say what's on my mind without actually saying it. Anyone who reads it will take their own interpretation of what it is about, and I get to have some sort of creative release. I don't even know why I'm writing this down. No one's ever going to read it. Maybe one day when I'm dead (watch, I'll die tomorrow) someone will read the poems and think they suck, or they're wonderful, or they won't know what to think. They are kind of superficial, not really earth shattering in their revelations; their grammar and style are to be improved, and not to mention that some need to be finished altogether. In the true style of a practicing procrastinator, I'll do it tomorrow.

—Morgan C. McCormack

Disclaimer

Contents of this anthology may not be suitable for all.

This anthology is a comedic look at really bad poetry written in teen angst years. It is not meant to indulge in, or support, senseless acts of violence that may have been written about in a poem. TeenAngstPoetry.com believes that the best expression of emotions comes through really bad poetry—not violence.

With the satirical nature of this book it may appear that some poems are making fun of depression; however, we realize how serious and damaging these emotions are. Nevertheless, **all submissions have been added because the authors have overcome their angst and they are able to laugh at their past and the products of their angst**.

Additionally strong language is used that may be offensive to some; nevertheless, all authors deemed the profanities as fitting to the expression of their angst.

Note: Most poems are more funny when read aloud.

Definition and Categories

Teen Angst Poetry is the poetry one wrote during adolescence when one is depressed or hurt. It is an outlet for "profound" thoughts (or you thought so at the time—as in "Yes! This explains everything I mean to say. This is my heart and soul on paper!"). Most often it has horrible rhyming schemes and very obvious metaphors.

Teen Angst Poetry has been divided in to twelve categories, which are:

Breakups (I will never love again poems)

More Than Like (Love poems)

I Am Alone (No one understands my pain poems)

Obvious Metaphors (Figurative language poems)

School (Poems about cliques and math class)

Life Sucks (And I want to die poems)

Fuck You (You don't understand me!/I hate you poems)

Political Action (Fight the power poems)

Pointless Ramblings (Poems with no meaning made up of words that sounded "good" together)

Odes (Poems to famous people like Kurt Cobain)

For Fun (Silly poems)

Other (Poems with self-appointed themes)

Breakups—"I Will Never Love Again" Poems

These were most often written when the authors were devastated because their **heart was broken** and to save their heart from ever feeling such pain they would vow to **"never love again."** The poem could be about the end of a three-year relationship with a high school sweetheart, or it could be about someone they barely know, but felt that they really shared something special with. These poems are jaded and **betrayed** in tone; they are about putting up walls so the authors could cocoon themselves in sorrow. This category also includes poems written about wanting to **break up** with someone but feeling a struggle in doing so.

Elliot Kyoto Marcus Johnson was my first love. I was in eighth grade. I was thirteen years old and every night, after my parents went to bed, I would call him secretly from the darkness of my room so no one could hear. He said I was his best friend and he had never felt about anyone the way he felt about me. . . . Until we went to camp with our middle school and he spent all night at the dance sitting outside talking with my best friend Caitlin. He broke up with me the night before our junior high graduation dance. He was supposed to be my date. He spent all night cuddled up with Caitlin on the couch. Two days later Caitlin said they were going out because "He doesn't like you anymore, and he likes me, so it doesn't help anyone if I don't go out with him." Thank you very much Caitlin Keeley. I was sure my heart would never heal again. So I wrote him this song . . .

Telephone Song
NICOLA SUMMER CORREIA-DAMUDE
(*A pleading ballad to Elliot Johnson*)

Verse 1

I thought our love would last forever,
In time.
Because my love was as a friend,
To you.
And now I wonder if you ever felt this way,
But in my mind I know you used to.

Chorus

So what happened

To the long nights,
On the telephone,
Making wishes on the stars that shone,
But never quite as bright
As our friendship did those nights,
I remember . . .
Why don't you?
Ieeeeeeel remember you. Ohhhhho You.

Verse 2
You let me search your soul
And I let you search mine.
It was amazing the great solace we could find.
And now I wonder how it is you let it die?
But I have to believe you wanted to try . . .

Chorus
So what happened
To the long nights,
On the telephone,
Making wishes on the stars that shone,
But never quite as bright
As our friendship did those nights,
I remember . . .
Why don't you?

Ieeeeeeeeeeeeeeel remember you! Ohhhhhhho You!
I remember youhoooooeeeeeeoooo Ah! I remember
Youhohoooo oowooowooowooowhoo . . .
Why don't . . . Youwhoooooooh?

The junior high graduation dance (betrayal night) was not my last heartbreak at the hands of Elliot Johnson. On my summer vacation that year I went on a road trip across the Maritimes with my parents which was sooooo lame. So I spent most of my time listening to the Cranberries *No Need to Argue* album on my Walkman, crying, and thinking about how it was possible that Elliot Johnson didn't love me anymore. Picturing him slow-dancing in HER arms. So, I wrote a letter. I poured my heart and soul into a thirteen-page, handwritten, tear-stained letter telling him how much he hurt me and asking him how this could have happened. How Elliot? How? Two days after I returned home from Nova Scotia I got a call from one of Elliot's friends, a dirty big-pant-wearing jerk whom I hated, and he quoted back to me all the lines from my letter that he thought were the funniest. Elliot had given his friends my letter to laugh at. I think I felt my heart die.

Rot and Die.

So . . . I wrote him this song.

Hurting

NICOLA SUMMER CORREIA-DAMUDE

Verse 1

When you trust somebody
More than anybody
It feels good (Bum Ba Ba dabada)
Feels gooooowood.

When you tell somebody
More than anybody

It's secure (Bum Ba Ba dabada)
Secure . . .

Chorus
Then he takes your heart and he runs away,
And you need him more than you could ever say, And you want
    to tell him,
What he did to your day,
But he's gone, he's gone, he goooooone away.

And your (Bum Ba Ba dabada)
Hurting . . .
Yes yooooour (Bum Ba Ba dabada)
Hurting

Verse 2
Then he takes your writings
And he puts them up
On the walls (Bum Ba Ba dabada)
It's not fair
And he makes you wonder
If he ever gave a damn at all (Bum Ba Ba dabada) Could
    Heeeeeeeeeeeee?

Chorus
When he takes your heart and he runs away,
And you need him more than you could ever say, And you want
    to tell him,
What he did to your day,
But he's gone, he's gone, he goooooone away

And your (Bum Ba Ba dabada)
Hurting . . .
Yes yooooour (Bum Ba Ba dabada)
Huuuuurururting.

> **Note:** A few years later Elliot and I became friends again, he really liked me and felt terrible about what he'd done, but I was over it and one night when he was at my birthday party someone asked me to sing so I played all the songs I'd ever written about him for the whole party and boy did he ever shrink in his seat! Don't mess with a girl with a guitar my dear! HA HA HA HA HA HA HA HA!

Written at age sixteen, after the loss of my first love, who I refused to commit to exclusively. He dumped my sorry ass after a four-month relationship. At first, I didn't take him seriously. We broke up and made up more times than I can remember, although, at the time, I did keep tabs on my wall calendar. This time was the last time, and when reality hit, it was not only surprising, but also shocking. It felt as if my heart had taken a leap out of my chest off of a twenty-story building and smashed into a zillion pieces, and no amount of glue could ever repair or hold it together ever again. I didn't realize that I was so into this guy until it was too late. I actually had collected a small vile of my blood, so I could write it out in blood with my calligraphy pen (fun with bodily fluids, he, he), but when I told him, he said he'd rather just take the vile of blood instead, and have the poem in ink. I wonder what he did with it?! Do you think he had some sort of a plan involving a voodoo doll that looks like me?

Broken Love Misery

GABRIELLA KRISS

I bleed for you,
From my heart,
I bleed for love,
I can't part.

I bleed for memories so sweet,
I can still taste,
Please forgive my heart that cheat,
I bleed for that with every beat.

Every night I dream of you,
Thinking you'll come back,
What a sad hope,
I fear the truth I lack.

How do I let go,
I've been trying,
Pain is all I know,
My eyes are crying.

Don't forget the day,
You burn this candle,
You're in my heart to stay,
You're more than I can handle.

I believe this was written during or after a breakup with one of many very, very crazy girlfriends. And we're not talking crazy as in "Oh, you so crazy" we're talking crazy as in "I think we should see other people and by other people I mean you seeing a therapist." This is also a period of time where I see myself as quite the poet; however, because of my attempt to be very deep and mysterious, I now have no idea what I was getting at with this. But it looks like I'm back on the Nine Inch Nails and Nirvana again . . . sigh . . . I think I use to be a very grumpy and cranky teenager. (Note the word "acme" in the poem is something that was in my word-a-day calendar which, I thought, would make me sound smarter . . . it means the highest or most perfect point.)

Untitled

Z. K. TAYLOR

I have ran out of death
And climbed to the acme
Yet I fall below sea level
Deeper and deeper
With nothing
And no one
The blackness grows
And is becoming great
To a new high
That is lower than
It all
I will kill if I do not satisfy these

Angers with pleasures
I don't know how but I
Will still fall
With nothing
And no one
Only darkness pouring
Into my heart like a
Winter chill
Help me

I did date the subject of this poem. For about two weeks in grade nine. Our relationship consisted of French-kissing, sloppily, behind the school at lunch. Sometimes after school, too, but never for too long because I had to make sure I was on that big yellow school bus on time. But from the words I chose, you'd think it was my one and only soul mate I was pining for! You see, he told me he loved me within the first week and then the following week he broke up with me—at the time, it was the greatest tragedy of opposites I had ever experienced! It was also one of my first encounters with those three little words that can light up your life or make for the best of high drama. Truth be told, the distance I mentioned in the poem, amounted to (maybe) twenty city blocks. And in reality, we never actually went out together outside of school. But in that moment, in those two weeks—he was Romeo. Which I suppose made me Juliet. Of course, at that point in my life I hadn't read the play yet—so there was no way I could have known at the time that this breakup was, in fact, not such a bad thing after all. Twelve years and reading some Shakespeare can really help put things in perspective.

Love doesn't just go away

ERIN MILLAR
October 1991

How happy was I?
More than you could ever know.
Life was a dream when I was with you—
What you told me,

I couldn't believe,

No matter what I wanted to hear,

I couldn't believe.

Was it true? . . . maybe . . .

Now I'll never know.

When you left, you took my heart—

It didn't feel right, we let the distance get the best of us,

All that time without you, I still cared.

Listening to an old record,

Looking out my window,

The words fill my ears and tears sting my eyes . . .

Love Never Dies

Over and over, dancing on my soul, reminding me of better
  days,

When I smiled, when I laughed,

And I was truly happy with you . . . did you lie to me?

Did you lie to yourself when you told me?

I know you would never hurt me (or would you?)

But I don't see, I don't understand—if what you said was true
  Why?

Love doesn't just go away

Love never dies—true love can never fade!

I was so happy.

More than you could ever know.

Oh! The lovesick teen puts pen to paper! It's funny; as I read it over, it almost sounds, in some places, as though this poem was written for someone I had a relationship with at some point. Like maybe I'm looking back on a love lost, reflecting on the blissful beauty that was present in my life for a time. Nope. Not only did I never date this particular boy, I don't think I ever spoke to him. We may have had to interact during a class discussion at one point or another, but there was nothing more to it than that. I should have called this poem "Ode to a Two Week Crush." Because that was the long, and very short of it.

Love . . . but only in my dreams

ERIN MILLAR
1992

Darkness falls and I see your face in my mind,
Eyes that sparkle when you smile, a look so kind,
From outside, the light of a tired moon creeps through my
    window,
I gaze out at the night so black, and I know,
That you're out there somewhere, although I can't see,
And maybe, just maybe, you're thinking of me.
I pull down the shade, and turn to my bed,
Your handsome face dominates thoughts in my head,
A wishful mind, the memories run,
Of the times we laughed in the light of the sun,
In my mind, my dreams, and only there,
Is where I know you really care.
With the rising of the sun comes dawn,

And my dreams of love with you are gone,
Swept away and reality looks me in the eye,
I see my wishes are in vain and begin to cry,
Or are they? Only you know,
I wish you would let your true feelings show,
But I don't know how you feel and for now that means,
I have love . . . but only in my dreams.

I don't know if I even dated the person I wrote this poem for/about . . . because I can't remember for sure who I wrote it about. We might have dated . . . or it might have been about a girl I had a crush on before I realized I was gay and came out of the closet. But it was my attempt at a rhyming poem.

Untitled
MICHELLE BJOLVERUD

I used to be the apple of your eye
But now it seems I'm just a sty
I can't say I miss your love
It must of been a sign from above
I've got to move on to better things
What we had I guess it was just a fling
So say goodbye to days of old
Because our blooming love has turned to mold

She would probably disagree if you asked her now. But good luck finding her, I never saw her again. Nevertheless, it was true. At the precise moment, on that April evening around midnight, when she spoke those three ill-toned words, a clap of thunder struck.

"We are over!" echoed in my ears as the sky broke open with preemptive tears.

I stood stunned, mouth gaping.

Should I have known this was coming? Some might say yes, some not. The truth was I had no idea. For in fact over the last six months I had been falling deeper and deeper in love.

But there I stood at the threshold of my parents' house getting soaked as she disappeared into her dad's banana-yellow Corvette.

I hadn't even uttered a word, not even a plea to wait. It was too late. She was gone in a flash, and I was left with Nature's cleanser—the rain. That space beneath my chest ached as if slashed by the sword of a samurai. There was nothing left to do, but wander. Yes, right then. Maybe you, too, have been in that precise place before—a good wander can heal many a cut.

And that was when the words to the poem flowed, with my tears.

Unicorn Pain II

GEOFFREY M. GLUCKMAN
June 1993

Deep gray holes of white
Envelop the half-moonlit sky.
Desperate needs drain my might.
Can our love overcome such a lie?

Is this blackest night to die?
Recede calm waters of blue
As salty drops erode our tie,
And hearts of unicorns shape our hue.

Contorted mass lies the carcass soul,
As distant days part our ways,
Yet throbbing sentiments take a toll.
And continues the tortured, twisted maze.

Return though our spirits must,
To accept the ultimate trust.
Other worldly steps on your soul,
May our love mark this six-foot hole.

This poem wasn't written with anyone in mind (that I can remember, at least). I never felt like I really needed someone to grow. I just needed them to have fun or feel accepted. But I grew without the aid of others. I think that the last few lines may have been something I originally called "the bridge." I still don't really know what a bridge is, but I knew then, and am still aware of the fact, that famous songwriters use them to "mix things up a bit." Perhaps that's what I was trying to do with this poem, mix things up a little bit, get away from the ABAB rhyme scheme, and write a hit song. Or, at least, the lyrics to a hit song. I'm sure . . .

Hey--a study in awkwardness

POLLY DICTEZ

Hey, why did you leave me?
Hey, why did you go?
Yeah, you fucking deceived me!
I needed you to grow!
Asshole, come back,
I guess I loved you.
I needed someone.
That someone was you.
You, you made my dreams come true.
Then you . . .
Then you left me.
Now I'm alone and afraid of the dark,
Hey, asshole, you sure left your mark.
Yeah, you fucking deceived me!

I needed you to grow!
So you listened to her?
Why should I care?
Now I'm alone and afraid of the dark.
Yeah, you fucking deceived me!
I needed you to grow!
As I lay and stare ahead.
The demons of revenge dance in my head.
But instead I'll beg and plead.
Help you overcome your fear and greed.
Hey, why did you leave me?
Hey, why did you go?

I wrote this poem shortly after a brief but tumultuous relationship with a hockey player named Kelly. He was short, blond, and had terrible body odor. I think the only reason I dated him in the first place was because he was a grade older than I, and I was awfully impressed with myself for having attracted an "older man." Several days after our breakup, I started seeing Kelly's best friend Ryan, whom I thought to be extremely attractive. It was quite the scandal . . . but I really should have known better. . . .

Portrait of a Player

CHRISTINE EAST
September 21, 1999

Before, I never saw you,
never knew who you were,
never saw through all the lies,
the gifts, of our love I was so sure.

I was wrapped in the illusion,
thought he saw the inner me,
he made me feel so special,
but it could never be.

His eyes had always lingered,
on my body for too long,
I knew but I denied it,
I just listened to our song.

My fears would drift away,
with his lips against my skin,
but I'll never be so stupid,
as I was to be with him.

Now it is all over,
he's got her on his arm,
just because I wouldn't fuck him,
oh, I'd love to do him harm!

Little does she know,
how he plays the game,
he only wants to screw her,
and then make her feel ashamed.

I really am not bitter,
best wishes to him I send.
I just hope he doesn't mind
that I'm dating his best friend!

As you can see, things didn't work out with Ryan either (see Christine's poem "Portrait of a Player"). Our relationship lasted maybe a couple weeks, and I'm pretty sure he never asked me out in the first place. . . . So it may very well have been an imaginary relationship. At the time, I considered him the great love of my life, and after losing him, resigned myself to eternal spinsterhood.

Ryan

CHRISTINE EAST
November 7, 1999

I gave you all I had inside,
I held your hand,
I helped you fly,
I gave you pleasure,
you gave me pain,
you told me lies,
but never again.
We're through with laughter,
we're through with love,
I'm through with you,
and that's because,
you broke my heart,
you left my side,
to be with her,
you let me die.
My heart was empty,
but now it's full,

I don't need you,
or the tricks you pull,
I don't need hurt,
I don't need pain,
I can be myself again.

At eighteen I had mastered the art of getting laid. But love was something I tried to avoid. The effects it had on me were devastating. Unless I was in control of the relationship, of my own feelings, I was sure to be unhappy more than less. Once again Jen swept into my life, filled with lust for me (and love she promised, too) and willing to make amends. Our affair was savage and perfect, and lasted almost one whole month. It left me bitter, and I swore off love, forever. This poem was my contract to myself; my unveiling of the Wizard; my reminder that love is a biological function designed to propagate the human race.

Since then, and against my better judgment, I've fallen in love many times over. Every time is wonderful and agonizing. I can't help myself. It's hardwired into me. Into all of us, I hope.

Love

HARICOT JONES

Love is a weakness of the mind
Overpowered by the heart
Which throbs until the soul is blind
And ready to be torn apart
And surely when the spirit's gone
Dissolved by Woman's fatal kiss
Upon the intellect would dawn
That ignorance is truly bliss
But some of you may disagree
Consider this your luck
For few does true love truly see
And many does it fuck.

This piece was written just after I had turned sixteen. I think I was sad because I didn't have the kind of romantic life that you see on TV or in the movies. So these are the words that left my pen. I was reading Pablo Neruda's work at the time, so you can see reflections of his writings in this.

Love Song

CANDACE DEFREITAS

I could sit here and write
A love song tonight
But it would never again be read
It wouldn't be heard or overplayed.

I could sit here and write a song about you and me,
How we would look at each other and just let it be.

I could sit here and list the sweet nothings you whisper in my ear,
The way you'd hold me and call me dear.

I could sit here and write about a love lost and a new one
    gained,
And how much the first left me with pain.

I could sit here and write about your sensual stare,
Or how you came after me only as a dare.

I could sit here and write a love song tonight,
But it would never again be read.

The gentleman significant to me in grade eleven was older than I, and he had won my respect by being smarter than me—or at least, smart enough not to acknowledge that I was clever. Such a feat, for I was bored to tears of people who assumed I could do anything and who worshipped the ground under my witty feet, impressed me enough to gain my love as well as my respect. Since he never acknowledged that I was "so smart," I set out to prove that to him, and on the way I discovered that there were better things in me than being clever. He was the first person to whom I admitted, "I did not understand that; could you explain it to me again?" and those words, I knew, changed me from one who was merely an arrogant memorizer to one who really wanted to learn. I had always thought I was lazy; then I realized that for him I was willing to work hard and try until I got it right.

Everyone else treated him with scorn, and assumed that he had no life and would never have a girlfriend or even friends. Then a friend of mine told me that he did have a girlfriend, and it was then that I realized that I was jealous, deeply jealous, and that I loved him as well as respected him. In Jane Austen's *Emma,* Emma Woodhouse learns that a gentleman who was flirting with her is actually engaged to another woman, and she exclaims, "What right had he to come among us with affection and faith engaged, and yet with manners so very disengaged!" When I read that line I recognized what I had been trying to say, though at the time I read *Emma* all but the last verse of the poem was already written. If I revealed to even my friends what I thought of him, I would become as mocked as he was. I did not defend his social life before anyone else who laughed at him, either, for I still do not know how true what my friend told me is, and I respect him too much to spread gossip. Hurt at my deception, and confused about my own knowledge of him and my own feelings, in my journal I wrote the first three verses of this poem, addressing him. It is more of a song than a poem, but I lack the skill to set the tune down.

A year passed, and, looking for submissions to this anthology, I came upon that poem and sent it, but it still was incomplete. It was after I had read another book, Peter S. Beagle's *The Innkeeper's Song*, that I found the inspiration for the last verse. In the book, two former apprentices of a great wizard known only as "our friend" talk of a stable boy who loves and worships them: "A good child. He is full of wonder and he really does work very hard . . . I suppose our friend has said exactly the same thing about us, many times. To whomever he loved."

The relationship between me and the gentleman concerned was closest to a sorcerer's apprenticeship, I had joked once. And I think he would say the same thing of me, "She is full of wonder and she really does work very hard."

I wish to him and whomever he loves: may your path be smooth and easeful, and may you have a good one and have untroubled dreams.

Do I Really Have To Tell You . . .

TAMARA

Do I really have to tell you how I feel when you walk by?
Can't you hear it in my voice and can't you see it in my eye
When I speak to someone else and yet my eyes are drawn to
    you . . .
And I hate to say so, but it's true.

Hasn't no one ever told you how I change when you are there?
How I smile and laugh more often, careless of all my care,
How our accidental meetings are all really set by me?
Are you truly that blind you can't see?

And why did you never tell me of that other girl you know,
Leaving me to walk unseeing when another told me so?
And she's yours and I am nothing, and I've lived a year's lie.
As far as you're concerned, who am I?

I'm a tangle of fears and angers—or I was until you came,
I was not completely human till you called me by my name,
And you found the best things in me, and I found the worst and
    rose above . . .
Go tell that to whomever you love!
Go tell that to whomever you love.

12:13 AM is mainly about having my heart broken. I was trying to be cynical about the experience but was still vulnerable enough to have feelings for someone. I was trying to be strong and tough. I felt that love was a weakness, that love was a drug I could become addicted to. I felt that my ex-boyfriend was the only person for me and that what I was feeling was basically overactive hormones and mild interest. I was trying to convince myself that I was "over" love. That the idea of it was old fashioned and not at all connected to my feelings or thoughts.

12:13 AM

NORAH ROLLAND
17 years old

12:13 AM
I come to YOU now
with the disease
of a dreamer
I come to you now
with regrets & warnings
not to give myself again
love, they say cannot be cured
it's never clean, it's never pure
can't you see I'm fading
I'm not as weak
as what you need
me to be
Friday I'm in love
but right now the DJ won't shut up

playing bad love songs
that seem so insipid
when you're sober
sorry baby I got off that stuff
just like he begged me to
addiction they say you cannot help
love is a narcotic
& I'm in rehab
the vampire who drank my blood
for 7 years or was it two
was my Romeo, my Prince Charming
but now it seems happily ever
after will never come true.

I broke up with my first boyfriend, James, because he cheated on me. I went away for the weekend and he made out with another girl eight hours after I'd left town. I was so hurt. We had been together for a month, which is forever in grade eight time.

I wrote this poem in between breaking up with James and getting back together with him. I think we were broken up for three days, during which he pleaded and begged for me to take him back.

And then I thought about it. . . . Well, there isn't anyone else that is interested in me. I like his friends. If I stay with him for a little bit more maybe I can become better friends with them. Maybe he *is* sorry for what he has done. Maybe he didn't mean to do it. So eventually, I did take him back, but then we broke up two weeks later when I dumped him for his best friend.

Yes, thirteen years old and I already knew how to play the game. {For more info on James, check out Sara's More Than Like poem.}

James Breakup Poem

SARA BYNOE

My eyes are going blind
glazed over and aglow
You say things that confuse my mind
Take you back?
I say NO!

My hurt did not leave
You took my heart

You are the thieve
My forgiveness you will not get
I wish, I wish we had never met

My emotions I will now keep
If I give them to you again
I know I'll weep

I'm closed up and alone
What I know now
I wish I had known
When the time comes you will pay
I wonder—just what you will say?

"Oh gawd, the pain, the pain of it all . . ." This one was a "Breakup about to happen" / "You stabbed me in the back" poem. This girl and this guy started spending a lot of time together and becoming really friendly . . . it was my boyfriend and my friend. Fucking ouch.

Even worse, I wrote this for my poetry project for English class. I remember coming into class late, trying to sneak in unnoticed, and it almost worked, but the clanking of my huge-ass three-foot metal wallet chain (remember those?) gave me away. Instead of getting into trouble for being late, the teacher started going on about my poems and how good my poems were . . . and then she read this one. Everybody must've known what it was about. It was hell. When she was done, I wanted the earth to open up and swallow me whole. Then the teacher said that I had "The Soul of a Poet." My ego was hugely flattered, but I was still excruciatingly embarrassed. If only the earth would open up and swallow me and my poor Poet's Soul.

Cold as Ice
SARAH F.

Let them have it
If that's what they want
Build a roaring fire
And leave me
Out of the circle
Where they warm their hands
And their hearts
Their close bodies

Cast shadows
Against the pristine snow
Where my own heart lies deep
Buried in an icy drift
I won't let them know
That I want in
And I won't let him know
That I'm jealous
Of the person next to him
I won't tell her that
She once made me feel
Warm
And the distance between
Them and me is
Frigid
But I'll surround myself
In crunchy snowflakes
And my heart is like a lump of
Ice
That radiates more chilly cold
Than the bleak white snow

Well, I think that this speaks for itself. It's a breakup poem, and it sucks. The boy in question simply stopped talking to me (how mean) and then had the brass-balled gall to go and talk shit about me. He went and told my own friends that I was "immature," "obsessed," and "annoying," and then went and told other people that I'd cheated on him! Very dangerous, considering that I had shit on him that was so much worse . . . SO much worse.

I was still blaming myself ("I suck! I Suck! Oh why must I suck so much?) and only beginning to become wrathful (Oh, You Suck!). So this is the midpoint—You *also* suck.

And you're probably wondering what the incriminating shit I had on him was—let's just say that some people (especially when drunk) take the expression "fucking the dog" literally. Damn, now that would have made for a good retaliatory bathroom-wall poem.

You Also Suck

SARAH F.
Grade 9, age 14–15

So fine then, I'm annoying
And I'm immature at best
I only irritate you
And I'm stupid and obsessed
But just 'cuz I'm pathetic
Did you have to be a jerk?
If only you were honest
We could have made it work
But the way that you ignored me was evil and unfair

You left me on a lifeboat that had long run out of air

So maybe I'm a loser and I'm not even worth a fuck,

But you acted really beastly

So you should know

You Also Suck!

This poem comes from a "collection" I started after my mom gave me a set of notebooks for Christmas—those red-and-black dollar store ones. I'm sure she was thinking I'd recount tales of My Little Pony and the Enchanted Castle or that I'd ooze sentiment about the oodles and oodles of boys that me and my friends fancied. I think she even put the caption: "May you fill these pages with joy and laughter. Love, Mom" at the start of one of them. But after much deliberation, I decided to give it a title that would reflect my true soul. I called it: Ultimate Loneliness: Tales of Divorce and Depression. I never did things half-assed. You see, you need a good title if you're going to get published. And I was going to be published. This was to be the start of the youngest published poet of my time with gritty outtakes on life in the midst of teenage torment. The critics were going to love it.

Needless to say, if this book had made it on the shelves (I'm sure you guessed that it didn't), then "Their Love" would have fit right in, as it's a poem about my parent's divorce and all. So Mom, if you're reading this, please know you are the one who loved us children. And if Dad's flipping through these pages, it was you.

Their Love
HEATHER TAYLOR
January 27, 1991

It was split apart
Never to come together
So they loved different people
And made many mistakes

They tugged at the possessions
Not caring for nothing
But taking everything
They broke others' hearts

One loved the children
While the other grew apart
But they hardly cared for each other
They hurt the children's hearts

So they live their lives apart
Trying to forget
The always ugly past
Where their love was never strong

"The Hit" was written after a particularly violent argument with a boyfriend who, I mistakenly thought, loved me completely. I escaped the relationship with bruises all over my body, stiff and sore and bleeding, and instead of going to the hospital or telling the police, I locked myself in my room and wrote a poem. Typical.

The Hit

K. BANNERMAN

Welcome to the smell of rotting fruit
Oh, sweetness,
I take a bite of your thigh,
Expecting heaven
And getting a mouthful of sand.
I cuddle into the warmth of your bruises
Purple, yellow,
And they listen delicately
To my breathing heart.
It's so hot
It makes my veins cling to me
Like sticky violet worms.
No hands alone now.

In the 1995–96 school year I knew three Jasons. There was Jason G. a good friend that I met at boarding school. Jason B. who was a self-proclaimed heroin addict who later set a hockey arena on fire and was charged with arson and who during court tried to blame it on me (but that's a whole other poem). And lastly, there was Jason N., who I was having a long-distance relationship with while in boarding school stuck in the middle of the parries.

I had intended this poem to be for Jason N. but it could be used, and was used, for any of the Jasons. This poem is best explained as a draw-and-tell story. So, please imagine the story as you go.

Jason
JOLEEN SADLER

I've been walking in this park for sixteen years
been through the hills and over my fears
I've never seen a person until that day
across the river, not a word we did say
through the river I tried to swim
got caught in the current and didn't reach him

Through the darkness and the grim
I never felt a feeling until I saw him
every organ in my body is being ripped out
and my happiness is being pecked by the trout

I tried to build a bridge to reach the other side
the wind from above and the water did collide

I flew through the air not feeling a thing
Flying through the air as though I had wings
My imagination took over while I was in flight
thinking that I'll make it to the other side completely alright
I fell in the water again and almost died
Came up for air, he just stood on the other side

Through the darkness and the grim
I never felt a feeling until I saw him
every organ in my body is being ripped out
and my happiness is being pecked by the trout

I never felt lonely until this day
I was tired of my park and I couldn't stay
so I climbed a tree and a branch across the water
He turned his back and left, I fell to my slaughter
He turned around and reached his hand to help me
but it was too late, I already fell from the tree
I fell in the water and reached the other side
He had already left, through all that I tried
All that was best for me was on the other bank
So I walked into the water and finally sank

Through the darkness and the grim
I've never felt a feeling until I saw him
every organ in my body is being ripped out
and my happiness is being pecked by the trout

I wrote this one after spending a drunken weekend with some guy friends up in Northern Saskatchewan. At the cabin, I met this guy who I really hit it off with, one of the first guys I'd ever met who I could talk with about something other than hockey and beer. I even told him I might be queer, which he thought was "cool." He was so indie rock cool, fun, and approachable but impossible to really get to know. He moved back to New Zealand the next day, I was totally heartbroken, really wishing I could cry or something but I couldn't.

Sayonara

JONAH ROBBINS

What makes for a goodbye?
Is it soft weeping?
Smiles of what never was?

What makes this magical pain?
This hard, inky treaty of
promises to write.

How can this exist?
Why does the ending of a nod,
The finish of a smile—
Why does this finality carry so many barbs?
Why is this pain distant from me?

Why this:

Why did I meet you so late?
Why this misopportunity?
Why this circumstance cutting off my pain?

Why to infinity?

I'll say this:
"See you Q-Ball."

More Than Like— Love Poems

These poems are not very angsty, but because they are often so horrible and were written in the teen years they still apply. Named after Sara Bynoe's "love" poem to her first boyfriend at age thirteen, **More Than Like** includes poems about **relationships** that actually happened or ones that were simply **daydreamed about**. Being young **love poems,** these are interesting because they are full of words like "forever, "always," and "**soul mate**." After growing out of this phase one can look back on these poems and feel very naïve, often producing the effect of regret and severe embarrassment. Sometimes these were written to make someone else happy (as in—fine—here's your damn **love poem**) or to get someone back into your life (I never meant to hurt you, come back), but all poems are about people who had a significant effect in the author's **love life**.

This is the first "love poem" I ever wrote. I was in grade eight, dating a guy in grade nine. I think he really should have been in grade ten, but he failed grade one or something. Apparently, he was quite the player because I was rumored to be girlfriend #572, but since we had lasted two weeks already, I knew that this was something serious. So, James and I are at the local amusement park, with a bunch of friends, having a great day. We're in line for the log ride with my best friend Sarah when he turns to me and says, "I love you."

Now, I'm thirteen years old, I know this guy is a player, and I'm not too sure how into him I am. I am dating him because we like the same music, he has cool friends, and he's the first guy to ever ask me out so, I say "thanks" and give him a kiss. I don't think I ever said it back to him—or at least not at that moment. This poem is what came out of me not knowing how to answer him.

Just so you know—because it is referred to in the poem—James was part of those modeling scams where they have a big meeting at a mall then hire on some suckers who are willing to pay money to get a portfolio, and to take classes to learn how to walk. At the age of thirteen I knew that it was a scam, but still it was cool to have a boyfriend that was a *model* even if everyone teased him about it.

The best thing that came out of dating James was that this was the beginning of my angst-filled teenage life and my career as a teen-angst poet. Thank you James for telling me you loved me after two weeks, and thank you for cheating on me two weeks after that.

More Than Like

SARA BYNOE

I wonder what you're thinking, so I ask
Are you contemplating things in your past?
I don't care about what you were
I don't care about your games
To me you are only James
You're kind, caring and fun
The list goes on until I am done
You're more than words can say
I don't think your modeling is gay
If you must know—I do like you
but it's more than like
It's not quite love
but it's more than like

PS: I must apologize for the immature use of the word "gay" in this poem. I was thirteen.

This poem never had a title until this anthology. I suppose at the time I thought the poem spoke for it-self, but now I find that I need to preface its horribleness with a disclaiming title: Pathetic Love Poem. This poem is about my high school sweetheart. We were together for three years. I wrote this poem around our eight-month anniversary. I'm sorry. I don't know what made us stay together for so long; per-haps it was love, perhaps it was friendship, perhaps it was need.

So, this boyfriend and I were into the all ages punk rock scene at the time (perhaps in the Emo clique or Hardcore, I'm not exactly sure). He was a musician with five bands and would write oodles of songs about me, except he would never sing them to me alone. The only time I got to hear them was at his gigs, which I went to every single weekend. Now, punk rock, for those of you that don't know, is very loud. The guitars are often so loud that they drown out the singing—so I hardly ever got to hear the lyrics he wrote about me. I was oh so sorry that I could not hear what he was screaming about me in some dirty community center in the bad part of town. I was so stupid and so sorry.

Now, almost ten years later, I'm just sorry that I let myself be so pathetic.

Pathetic Love Poem

SARA BYNOE
December 3, 1995

I'm sorry I can't understand what you're trying to say
I try so hard to make out your messages
Interpret your songs

Sometimes I'm too nearsighted and I only see what's closest to
the top
I'm sorry I talk too much
Am I scaring you to shut your mouth?
I'm just trying to cover the silence—paint it over with my voice
But it wears too thin and holes begin to form
I'm sorry I can't patch them
I'm sorry I feel uneasy when you talk about your past
I wish I was your only
But I guess I've had a past, too
I'm sorry I should have waited for you
I'm sorry I'm insecure
I'm sorry I sometimes act unsure about how you feel
Maybe I just want to hear you say it
When you say it makes my heart melt
When we kiss—I've never been kissed so sweetly
I've never been held so tenderly
I've never been in love
I'm sorry if you may have
I'm sorry that I'll lose you one day
I'm sorry that will hurt
I'm sorry I trust you—and tell you everything in my mind and
soul
I'm sorry that it bores you
I'm sorry—I'm sorry
I only aim to please you
All I want you to do is love me

Grade seven. Larkin was my first kiss, and my first French kiss (and he was very good for his age). We were together for a whole month, which is years in jr. high time. Everyone thought that we would get married. I cannot remember the circumstances for writing the poem but I'm sure they were heartbreaking.

Untitled

JOLEEN SADLER

Love cracks
Love breaks
but sometimes it can be sewn together
when it is together it can never break
forever and ever and ever

So I had been in love with (read: lusting over) this unattainable person for, well, it seemed like an eternity, but it must have been a few months. It was getting to the point where I was going to explode if I didn't somehow miraculously wind up alone in a room with him. The only problem was that I had been "testing the waters," so to speak, and only got lukewarm to downright chilly responses. Having dealt with my share of unrequited feelings, I wrote a sort-of "pre-apology" for (as I pictured in my mind) bombarding this person with my lips. I remember thinking I was sooooo clever for not entirely revealing what the "gift" was. Though the title is totally un-PC, at that point I found it inconceivable that my kiss could be returned.

Impossible Indian Giver

MORGAN C. McCORMACK

I have something to give you
But I know you'll hate me when I do
Please don't get the wrong idea
Your wrong impression's what I most fear
This gift is a gift that you cannot return
But if you return it, my wet lips will burn
You've got to know just how I feel
You have to know, you're my Achilles' heel
To purge my sin is not enough
The gift must be given off the cuff
It will surprise the hell right out of you
And I know you'll hate me when I do.

At the time this was written, I was hopelessly in love with my best friend and also hopelessly in the closet. Once she got a boyfriend, things began to get a bit tense and I would start to throw little jealous fits—this poem being the result of one of them. I don't know what I was thinking, however, because in a fit of self-censorship and in order to "hide" who it was that I was talking about, I played the "pronoun game" and changed all indications of gender from masculine to feminine. The idea was to make it appear as though I was addressing some boy, but when I read it now, it just sounds like a cringe-worthy Melissa Etheridge rip-off.

#10
MORGAN C. McCORMACK

Can she make root beer come out your nose when you laugh?
Can she make you kiss her on a dare?
Does she understand the gravity of the situation?
Or does she even care?
Will she be there when you come crashing down?
Will she make you truly happy?
Does she even understand you the way that I do?
Or does she feel that sappy?
I can only sit and watch
I can only pray
From my secret hiding spot I watch her act the play.

When I was sixteen, I found this group of friends, and we all were fed up with the high school scene of parties and dating and popularity. Instead, we created this tribal, spiritual brotherhood thing, which often involved mushrooms, saunas, cabin trips, and sneaking around the small city we lived in and climbing on top of buildings to smoke pot and hang out. These friends meant everything to me, they were all smart, funny, adventurous, warm, affectionate straight guys. And I was just finding my way out of the closet, and into love with them. Big love. Desperate, on my knees love disguised as brotherhood and every little gesture and conversation I would document, hoping I could fall in love with them. I wrote this poem one night at my house, just hanging out with my boys, one who'd just had a breakup, one who understood my emotional pining and one who I really really wanted to notice my emotional pining.

Try a Little Tender . . . ness

(inspired by the Song by Otis Redding)
JONAH ROBBINS

Jason is soft. He feels.
Tender.

I sing, I feel music.

Landon reads catalogues of naked women.
He is shallow.

Taylor sleeps.
Bitterness has bitten his soul.

That bitch, that foul bitch.
I want to reach out.
And I know I can.
I have love, I have truth.

Part of that is Jason.

This is a poem I wrote to a friend whom I was secretly in love with. Because he wouldn't sense my secret love for him. I wrote searing poems about how he was ruining the "friendship brotherhood." We'd hang out, and I'd yearn to talk about my feelings and he'd talk about normal stuff, like what he had on his sub or how he wanted to get a set of turntables.

And So It Goes

JONAH ROBBINS

In the hand of friendship,
　　　You are a hangnail of discontent.

In the flood of brotherhood,
　　　You are a trickle of negativity.

"I dreamt in French last night," you say.
Oh yeah? "I dreamt I kicked your ass last night."

Oh, Stupid *Chris*. That's what I call him now. Well, *called*, before I was over it but after I was obsessed with it. With him. Chris was the most girlish-looking, wide-eyed boy I've ever known. Girls liked him, really liked him, but as he lived in some small Alberta town, I did not see him very much. Chris hitchhiked everywhere (god only knows the things that could have happened to him—or maybe they did happen—if a big, burly truck-drivin' man pulled up to the side of the road to let in this attractive specimen of fresh-faced youth). I hadn't seen a boy naked before. I hadn't felt a boy's hardness before. Eventually, I felt Chris's.

I think becoming a teenager is signified by the unbelievably long phone conversations you begin having. Sometimes Chris and I had three-hour phone calls—and always starting at midnight. Our girly-boy heartthrob made me feel something, and now—with the benefit of age—I can see that I made him feel something, too. I made him feel important. Because, crush as he was of mine, he was privy to certain information. Information about me, about the terrible times I was going through. He asked me for details about cutting myself. You know you've hit the jackpot when you have a tendency to self-mutilate, and then who should pop up but a boy who enjoys all the gritty details. Think of the attention, girls! Perhaps that's too harsh of me. I don't believe he enjoyed the details as much as he enjoyed playing the savior. Ugh. Nothing makes you feel good like being part of a walking, talking cliché.

He had black leather gloves, obviously. And I can still call up the smell of them. I loved it. On a quiet winter night, all sound muted by the snow, atop the rock at my secret place he would hold me and I would revel in the magic of it. Freezing but found. I'm not embarrassed at how carried away I got—all roads pointed to my

thrilling to his black-leather-gloved touch. It's the obsessing after
the fact, that deep-down groaning mass of sickness in your stom-
ach, an emotional pain akin to the physical one of cramps, that I
could have done without.

Untitled

MELINDA GIDALY

I long for the sweet touch of a boy
gone wrong
the tormented torturous tumultuous
soul
with black leather fingers reaching
out
for something dark yet sweet & succulent
&
not quite
forbidden
foreboding
I long for the smell of your gloves
& your fingers in my hair
only
you're not
you're not wrong
you are not right
you are the middle boy
the middle ground
maybe it is you who longs for the
misconstrued shock of a girl gone wrong's

fingertips
her tacky torment
just as real
& just as painful
perturbed disturbing
the fresh taste
makes haste
in the face
of an almost joyously dark place
but not quite
o
your fingers in your gloves
are a little more frightening
than mine in that
soft
black leather
of the world

This poem was written when I was sixteen and a junior in high school. I wrote it for my boyfriend (who is now my ex-husband), but I was afraid of how I felt. I wasn't sure if what I was feeling was truly love. Now after three marriages and attaining the ripe old age of forty-two . . . lol . . . I still am not sure I know about true love. The only love I know for certain is the love that I see shining in my daughter's eyes.

Untitled

KIM A.
1978

I can't say I love you
'Cause I never learned how
Except for my teddy bear
(but that's not quite the same somehow).
Yet you tell me you love me,
And I know its true
(and I know I feel like you do, too).
And although I'm not sure,
perhaps . . . ,
I guess . . . ,
I must really,
honestly,
love you, too.

I was extremely angry when I wrote this. My boyfriend at the time really managed to piss me off to the point where I wanted to hurt him in the worst way I could think of. It used to be that when I got angry, I got to the point where I could no longer stand it, and I would just burst into tears. This was one such occasion . . . and I thought if I didn't love him so damn much, I wouldn't be so full of rage.

SCARS

GABRIELLA KRISS

The salt in the tears,
Bloody bruises,
And meaningful prayers.

Hate is love,
Anger is love,
Revenge is love,
Pain is love.

At sixteen, during the peak of my groupie years, I happened on a date with a drummer named John, from a Canadian band. It was surprising, and refreshing to be treated like a lady.

Most guys in bands thought they were hot shit and treated me like some kind of play thing. John was very nice, and polite. Our evening together was quite romantic. We met at his autograph signing session at A&B Sound. He wrote, "I love you, I really do!" on my poster. I left the store, and went back to get another thing signed for a friend which my friend and I forgot about. John sent a guy to look for me, and soon we started chatting and he asked me if I wanted to have dinner with him. We took the bus back to his hotel, and hung out in the courtyard, where he asked for permission to kiss me. I was in complete awe with this gentle drummer. Later we went to his room, ordered pizza, and just talked and kissed all night. A few days later, on a rainy night, I was reminiscing about my night with John, in the darkness of my bedroom, and wrote this poem.

SOLITARY

GABRIELLA KRISS

I'm curled up in a sweater,
Nice and cozy,
But, without you,
It's so lonely.

The sweater's so huge,
It fits my whole body,

Rain's pouring down,
So hard from above me.

It's dark, except for candlelight blinking,
Thinking about you, I feel my inside twisting,
I want to be with you . . . ,
To your heart, I'd be listening.

It's so scary,
Not knowing.
Do you really feel,
What you're showing?

Well she was hot! And I had a big crush on her all summer long but never could tell her so I wrote her a song. It was my very first song accompanied by piano. I learned how to play the piano just for her. You should hear it with the piano; it's quite good.

She was the type who liked cool, good-looking men, who I equated with being "spontaneous" because they are always doing cool, stupid things. I was not. Hence I'd be there to clean up her fright. Which is my favorite line of the song because it rhymes "fright" with "fight." Another favorite line is "It was real 'cause my feelings don't lie." That's true, except with this girl 'cause she never gave me the time of day. But I did give her a tape with the song on it at the end of the summer. So maybe one day she'll play it for you.

Chance

JOSH EPSTEIN

Age 17

Verse 1

I'm not your ordinary lover, I'm not expecting you to stay
But if you gave me my chance, I'd never let you turn away
'Cause when I saw you that day, I knew you were worth the fight
And everything you said sent me a-soaring
And it was real 'cause my feelings don't lie

Chorus

And I'm not asking you for the rest of your life
And I'm not asking you to make love to me tonight
I'm not even looking for a little summer romance

All I want is a chance
All I want is a chance

Verse 2
So you think I'm not spontaneous
But what about putting up this fight
Spontaneous will leave you when it gets rough
But I'll be there to clean up your fright

[Chorus repeats until song and love fades out.]

The year was 1990, he was a camp counselor named Tod Omotani, and I was fifteen years old. One look at the guy and I was hooked—his undercut hair matching my own, I felt that he was my destiny. I ran back to my tent, whipped up the poem, and set it to music; what better than teen angst but teen angst brought to life with the Holy Trinity of Rock chords A, C, and G?

It could be attributed to the fact that it was a church camp, or perhaps that I was (back of the hand to forehead style) dramatic but, upon completing said poem I experienced a religious epiphany: Tod *had* to hear this song, he *had* to hear it from my mouth, and he *had* to hear it tonight. So there I was, set up with my guitar under his bedroom window, singing my heart out quietly, albeit intensely. It was like a Romeo and Juliet role reversal, and I felt so proud to be a pioneer for teenage girls everywhere with bleeding hearts.

While this singing was going on, I felt certain, in my black-clad-nose-pierced heart that Tod was just inside the window, falling madly in love with the mysterious musician who was generating such intoxicating music, and would, surely, come outside to take me in his arms and blah blah blah blah.

It turns out he wasn't in his room at all.

On the upside, his roommate couldn't get to sleep thanks to my enchanting voice. If Tod wasn't able to hear it, at least I could ensure that someone else was as unhappy as I.

Untitled

REBEKAH GRAYSTON

At times, you feel as though you're flying
And in the end you know you'll end up crying
But you know that I am here for you
I'll give you love to get you through
And so you won't end up denying
The love we have and have always had
I'll see you through the good and bad
But leave me now and I'll be forever dying
Forever dying
Forever dying

I Am Alone-and No One Understands My Pain Poems

These are very **depressed** poems. They are about feelings of **isolation,** not fitting into society, not having a peer group, and feeling as though there is no one in the world who has ever felt as **sad** as the author does at that moment. The image is: wallowing in **self-pity,** poems written on tear-stained paper in a dark room with candles burning, perhaps while listening to **sad music** fueling the angst, such as Sarah McLachlan or NIN.

It was Valentine's Day and all my friends went out without calling me. I was devastated and alone. I just got my driver's license that week and wanted to go out BAD. When I exhausted the idea of the phone ringing, I borrowed the family car and took a long ride by myself to the railway tracks. Parked under a grove of trees and wrote three poems. This was the first one finished at 11:17 PM, February 14.

Untitled

PAUL ANTHONY
February 14, 1992
Age 16

SITTING HERE, ALL ALONE
I COULDN'T SCREAM IF I TRIED
DON'T KNOW HOW I FEEL
JUST KNOW IT'S NOT RIGHT
TONIGHT I'M MY OWN VALENTINE

Wow. This one hurts on so many levels. I don't really remember what this one is about, and the odd thing is that at the time I wrote this, I think I had a boyfriend and wasn't alone at all. And the "screams in the night," I think those were intended to be metaphorical, nonauditory screams. You know, the screaming of my *soul*. I was being deep. Go with it.

Sometimes Alone

MORGAN C. McCORMACK

sometimes
alone
sadness is alright
sometimes
alone
screams rip through the night
sometimes
alone
I am still with you
sometimes
alone
I can still feel you
one time
together
I was not so sad
one time
together
there was no need to be mad

This poem was written in a dark room, lit only with candles, on tear-stained paper. This is my journal entry from that day:

Fucking horrible day . . . After school we had a dress rehearsal for the school play, it went horrible. Oh well. Dad picked me up and I asked if I could go to the video store, he had a spaz—I'm so sick of him! So whiney and stressed. I am so close to swearing at him. He doesn't have to take it out on me! Then I found out that Brett (my crush) has a girlfriend. Argh! But, I'm getting over it. Oh well, why would anyone want me anyway? I'm feeling really low . . . I found out that Jon (my ex) might be dating this girl, Angie . . . I don't have any reliable friends. I'm so bottled up, I'm going to explode any second. . . .

Well, it's a good thing I wrote this poem—so I didn't explode.

January 20, 1997

SARA BYNOE

I wrap my arms around myself
I feel so small
Once I was huge
Minute little creature that I am
Unworthy of any comfort
I deserve all I've got
Still I remorse
Hot tears fall down

Hell's water carries me away to a
Place with no dreams or friends
Right where I am
I go no where
I had hoped
Now I hope never to again
Wishing only hurts
Dreams only crush

At thirteen years old, I was fat, asthmatic, and wore jogging-suit sets. Of course, like all good teenagers, I found a poem in it.

Yes . . . I was that girl they stereotype in bad American teen movies—the one who eats lunch by herself in the corner. Usually this is the girl who, when you fast-forward out of high school and college, is beautiful and famous and all the jocks who laughed at her are mechanics with beer bellies who are saddled with ten kids and a ditzy former cheerleader weighing five hundred pounds. Unfortunately life doesn't work that way—I had to actually experience it.

I'm sure I was a bit paranoid about people actually moving from the benches I was sitting on and laughing to each other and I'm sure I was a bit surly as a result. Of course, sitting in my room and eating blocks of cheddar and boxes of crackers as I read Sweet Valley Highs and Harlequins by the hundreds, didn't help me too much. (NB: No wonder my view on love is skewed and cheese makes me queasy.) Neither did my evil gym teacher, who told my class the reason I didn't run cross-country was because I was allergic to air. Then again, without this life-altering material, poems like "Tears" would have never been written. Thank God for that.

Tears

HEATHER TAYLOR
January 27, 1991

They cry on others who cry with them
While we pity them for how they look

72

But even if she doesn't look like her mother
They cry

They cry for others who are like them
And who can't help looking like they are
While the outside laughs at them
They cry

They cry for themselves
And the yesteryears
Which reflects on their children
They will always cry.

This seems to be a bit of a reoccurring theme in my fat-sweater-wearing poetry days. Perhaps I felt . . . um . . . isolated from the rest of the world? But quoting myself from one of my own angsty poems, I can pretty much sum up my own feelings: "I do wish I could be answered but who would?"

Untitled

HEATHER TAYLOR

Alone
On the outside of them
Their laughing faces peering out of the world
Hearing their laughter
Trying to forget
While a hole surrounds
While a black hole surrounds
A black hole of sadness

Alone
In a world of no one
Forever feeling tears
And a hopeless tugging of the heart
Always trying to hide it in a world
A world of pain

Alone
Under many burdens
Struggling through nothing

While feeling their hate
Always trying
But forever looking above and seeing no end
No end to the suffering pain.

My sister and I got into a fight (as usual). She was telling me things like: "You're adopted," "You're ugly," and "You're a brat." I thought my sister was the coolest so I went into my room, cried, and wrote a poem.

Untitled

JOLEEN SADLER
April 30, 1991

I'm crying in my room and nobody cares
with a pain inside of me that I can't even bare
I'm that brat girl that cries every day
but this time it's not to get my way
I'm a burden and wish I was never born
instead be a goose with a loud blowing horn
who could fly away and be left in silence

This was written in the first month of university. Most of my friends had gone to other universities out of town, I had a hard time meeting new people since I did not live on campus, and one evening I just grew so lonely for my old life in high school that I wondered why did I graduate anyway and think that university is so great and everything? Some people I knew had stayed for an extra year in high school, so I was wondering why I didn't. I have since settled down, I love my program of studies, I have found some friends, and I do not miss high school so much (there are definitely perks to having only fifteen hours of class a week and not having to wake up early every morning) but I still am not very involved in the extracurricular life at university.

Graduation

TAMARA

Why did I break from bud and shell
For tales of seeing the sun arise?
Why did I trade my native hell
For any dreamland paradise?
There was no way I could remain
And not depart when so I'm meant—
A child in the womb retained
Poisons the same as excrement.
It's growing up, now meet its sorrow,
Knowledge you thought a pretty toy,
So know so much about tomorrow
Today no longer brings you joy.

You are not of them, though among them;
The people-place is not your own,
The halls are lovely, but along them
You smile at others, walk alone.

I wrote this poem the summer after I had gradu-
ated from high school. So many of my friends were
going off to college, university, or traveling. I felt
left behind and lost in a place I couldn't get out of. The
lines "I don't want to be a whisper / but I don't have a choice / I
wasn't born with an angel's voice" refer to my feelings of helpless-
ness and fear of growing up. "There's a virus raging in my veins / &
a poison that tries to escape" allude to my shame of having my
father's blood in my veins. This poem was also written when I was
very lonely and I felt that love was something that I didn't deserve
and that I would never find again. It was about being in a dark
place and feeling safe there.

My Fury & My Worries

NORAH ROLLAND
Age 18

poison escaping each facet
finding friends slip away
cos they have more
& I find myself alone like before
pensive with a pencil
I suppose I'm sinking in this sorrow
misery doesn't feel so bad
it's righteous feeling sad
blisters have turned to scars
I guess I went too far
trying to win this war
what am I fighting for

I don't want to be a whisper
but I don't have a choice
I wasn't born with an angel's voice
I fear my dreams will never come true
& I'm afraid the rain won't stop, too,
there's a virus raging in my veins
& a poison that tries to escape
but I can't explain
my fury & my worries
I carry my sorrow like a sword
& I'm still raising hell
cos there's a story I must tell
I dwell in a dungeon
waiting for prince charming
gathering an army
to make sure no one will harm me
yes I know I'm paranoid
are you unaware of the void
the emptiness eating me inside
the abyss in which I hide
rough tissues upon my broken face
each miserable day is a waste
I'm withering away in this place
I'm a whisper of a petal
resigning that I've lost this battle.

It is hard to recall just exactly what I felt when I wrote this poem in high school. I don't think I've ever had that feeling before or since then. I was having an off day, and I was feeling apathetic; kind of empty. I was bitter about something. I was trying to make sense of what I wanted. I think I was convinced that there was something seriously wrong with me mentally. Mostly, I think it was caused by typical teenage hormone imbalances.

BLACK FILLING

GABRIELLA KRISS

Can't find what it is,
But, it s on my mind,
Something I must miss,
To life, I feel blind.

Something is wrong,
With my empty mood,
Blackness of my soul is nude.

Blackness is pitch,
Of rotten sorrow,
I am rich,
Of the shit I swallow.

Where is my wrong?
The days grow long,
With everlasting misery,
My heart and mind disagree.

It's Friday the thirteenth again, only this time it's 2004. It does *not* seem like it was eight years ago that I wrote this.

This piece is less eye-rolling, albeit only slightly, because the focus is a little less woe-is-me and a little more searching-for-answers. Maybe that's what makes teen angst poetry so easy to mock: There isn't any active interest in searching for solutions. It's all about how awful and terrible things are for the person who wrote it. I speak for myself, of course.

The struggle to actually get off my tuckus, stop kvetching, and do something to change my circumstances is pretty apparent here. I always felt that urge . . . but not enough to follow through. That took a *lot* of time. I wonder if readers picture an emerging adolescent in these words. Sadly, that ain't the case, folks. In December of 1996 I was newly eighteen years old—an age I was desperate to avoid. As I like to put it, I was seventeen for three years!

I've recently discovered this is not uncommon: A February 2004 study found that one in four older teenage girls will suffer at least one major depressive episode within the next four years. The lead author of the study (Nancy Galambos of the University of Alberta) said that the level of depression she and her team found among girls in their late teens was quite unexpected. A *quarter* of the girls between sixteen and seventeen experienced at least one major depressive episode within that four-year period. Personally, I believe the number is likely to be even more.

Other studies report that girls who are sexually active and gals who smoke pot are more likely to suffer from depression, but as with all of these things, there are exceptions to every rule. I didn't have anything remotely resembling sex until I was at least twenty. And I wouldn't know how to inhale any kind of smoke without choking to death even now. I was never "cool" enough to do either of these things. How lovely to be twenty-five and able to celebrate my sometimes-dorkiness.

Untitled

MELINDA GIDAIY
Friday the 13th, December 1996

boys with greasy hair
  singing about girlfriends
    they don't have

or maybe they do.
  suffer for your art
suffer through your heart

what if she wanted
to sing? what if she
wanted to paint?
what if she thought she
could be
    all that you ain't?

sipping slurpees
  lounging fluorescents
these are the things
  I am made of

I could say this poem is just about wishing my friends would call more often. It's not. Really it's about falling in love with my best friend, fooling around with his ex-girlfriend, telling him, making him really mad, and waiting around all summer for him to call me back so I could apologize to him and we could get back to driving around, smoking Export A's, drinking beer on my parents' porch, listening to good indie rock, and hugging so I could smell his Old Spice deodorant and the Dep Gel in his hair.

Bitch Goddess

JONAH ROBBINS

The phone Is a goddess.
I kneel before her fat, malicious smile.
I plead with her, beg with her to
Bring me information, news, plans.
I use her, gratuitously.
I fondle her, stroke her, hum
Into her earpiece.
She thanks me by farting busy signals.
She twirls her grimy cord between her thick fingers.
She reaches down,
Plucks a string of drool off my chin.
It lolls down her finger.
Maliciously, she slurps up
My saliva, relishing my pain,
Master of my solitude.

Obvious Metaphors—Life Is a Mountain, a Road . . .

These are also awful poems. The young authors of these poems were trying to apply techniques they learned in English class. Most often, they play with **metaphors**, but these poems can play with **alliterations**, word charts, or **onomatopoeia**. These poems are obvious because their metaphors are either **cliché** or simply awkward. They are pretty easy to figure out now—but when you wrote them you thought that you were being so **deep**.

"I am a Rose" was written at my mother's house, which was in a part of the city that my friends did not live in. I was alone, and no one understood my pain. I was looking at a dried-up rose that I had in my bedroom as part of my decorations when I wrote this poem. You could say it was my inspiration.

I am a Rose

SARA BYNOE
November 2, 1993

I am a rose
With soft red petals at a glance
But there are those that choose to see the thorns
I have been dried up and hung upside down
My color has changed
My leaves have fallen off
Hung upon the wall
To gaze at but never to touch to smell to be thought of as some-
    thing beautiful
Now I'm gone
Thrown out because
My time has passed
No longer needed
My sweet scent has disappeared
And left the stench of a life of wonderment now taken to starva-
    tion to rot

It's funny, I remember writing this. I remember sitting on the pink carpet in my bedroom, leaning against my bed, and scrawling "My Body" down as fast as possible. But I don't know WHY I wrote it, or why I wrote it so desperately. The journal that it's written in is ripped, frayed, coffee stained, and smeared with some rusty-colored substance that might be blood. Perhaps that has something to do with it. Perhaps I had a massive paper cut, and needed to complete my creation before I bled out.

My Body

K. BANNERMAN

Welcome to my body, dear
It's not much of a temple, really. Just
A one-room shanty with a
Yard out back
A fire in the hearth and
Duct tape holding up the windows.
It's haunted, too.
I'm the ghost that walks its corners.
Gliding through cracks in the walls.
I'm the wind that whistles in the chimney.
I'm the creaking floor.

There isn't actually much of a story behind this poem,
except that the name of the person who inspired it
means "broad meadow" . . . it seemed profound at the
time. Really, I was just good at turning even minor relationships into
crises.

I THOUGHT

JAN KRISTY

I thought so much trusted
without knowing how much
and now this—
that I couldn't deceive myself
about my own independence,
proud detachment—
all these delusions
crumbled by someone as gentle as you,
and completely
by your simple absence of actions
or words
you did nothing
why did you do nothing?
you were a calm harbor
off a wild uncertain sea
you were the broad meadow
I could rest in,
close my eyes
and drowse in the sun
and now you've stolen away

like day
and left me to wake in the cold
you were the cave I could hide in
you were the broad meadow
I could rest in

This poem is fairly self-explanatory.

Untitled

JAN KRISTY

I thought I'd found a place
to hibernate

maybe it was selfish

I can't stand
seeing 2 people sharing an umbrella (isn't it an exquisite
    metaphor?)

I've been unable
to find a good metaphor
for simple loneliness,
for the old words "I miss you"

I guess being
a happy dormouse
would've been too easy—
sleeping away the winter blasts

I'm sure I'm stronger for this
and it must be good for me
like getting cavitied teeth drilled
or wisdom teeth pulled
(now why would you do that?)

Coming to terms with the guilt of being the dumper in a situation where lack of love was not the cause of the breakup. Pain was inevitable for both sides, but the guilt of initiating it really, really sucked. On the other hand, guilt is never a good reason to stay in an unfavorable position, since one can never please everyone. The least I could do for myself was cut the chains, and try to follow what was in my heart, but like with everything else, there was a price to be paid. I was tired of avoiding the obvious for the sake of sparing the dumpees' feelings.

TIRED

GABRIELLA KRISS

I feel like Atlas,
Holding up the world,
The world that has become yours.

I want you to be happy,
But, it's a high price to pay,

I don't want to drop your world,
Your soul,
That is mine also,
So precious,
That I love so dearly,
To be smashed.

I am strong enough,
To feel my pain,

But, too weak to feel yours,
Ours.

My arms are so . . . tired . . .

This poem came hard on the heels of my "Spice Girls"–induced, love-lost, men-are-pigs, Girl Power phase. . . . A very scary, self-righteous time accompanied by a bad hair cut and clothes I'm ashamed to admit I wore at the age of fourteen. I remember thinking myself so clever for coming up with what I considered to be a masterpiece of metaphorical poetry . . . Oh my.

Flight

CHRISTINE EAST
April 7th, 1999

I unfurl my wings
and set to the sky,
soaring free,
flitting high.

Then slyly you come,
over glen and dale,
I'm set in your sights,
your shot will not fail.

Your love, like a pistol,
sends a bullet to my heart,
I struggle and cry,
from the sky I depart.

You find me and hold me,
love coursing your veins,

you heal my wounds,
but my fear still remains.

You clip my wings and tame my mind
to keep me as your own.
You set me in a lust-wrought cage,
possession is my home.

Spring has come,
the lilacs grow high,
but I remain trapped in your heart.
Although the sky's blue
and the grass is now green,
my world is becoming night dark.

Fueled only by fear,
fearful only of you,
I set my mind free,
and decide what to do.

I'm taking back my wings,
relearning how to fly,
breaking from this cage,
and taking to the sky.

I've escaped to my freedom,
I'm flying far away,
I am independent,
can't steal my flight away.

The scene: Creative Writing 12
1. The assignment: Metaphor
2. The inspiration: that hideously large industrial-strength three-hole punch that you find in every classroom in every high school you've ever been in. I simply selected a random object in the room to write about, turning the familiar chunk of metal into an outlet for my oh so glorious bubbling angst.

Hole Punch

AMANDA MARIER
September 4, 1996

Slivery thin,
Razor sharp,
Perfectly circular,
Snowy white
Discs.
The cold iron beast lets out a piercing metallic scream as it
Opens its tawny jaws
To create
These lethal-edged circles.
Cutting them away
From the field
Of white they lived in.
Lived invisibly.
Lived peacefully.
Unaware of their future,
Of what fate held in store.

In all honesty I don't remember what class this was written for, only that the assignment was to write a piece that did a 180-degree turnaround and ended up at the opposite of where it started.

At that time in my life I was making those horrible realizations about certain career goals being impossible; for example, you can't be an archaeologist if you get Cs in science. The ensuing angst-ridden drama resulted in quite a few little rays of sunshine like this one.

Frozen Rain

AMANDA MARIER
May 1995

When I was small
And new,
I was a fresh snowflake
Falling through a moonlit sky.
Whole, sparkling, singular,
Yet intricate.
Delicate.
Now I have become
An icy white snowball,
Smashed on the hardened gray pavement.
Cold, shiny, packed hard.
Made up of too many sparkling snowflakes
Crushed together
To reach full potential.
Finished.

I wrote this poem when I was about sixteen or seventeen years old. The truth is that I don't' remember who I wrote it about. That just goes to show you how the things that seem to be important at one point in life become so insignificant at others.

Untitled

CANDACE DEFREITAS

He is like a rose
Beautiful, but with thorns
That can make you bleed.
He is a man
Looking out of a tinted window
But never allowing anyone to look in.
He is an emotional schizophrenic
Not sure whether to laugh or cry;
Thinking of what's between
When we live and die.

I was fourteen when "two faces" was written and I had just been dumped by my group of friends because they believed popularity could be theirs if only they could drop the dead weight, me. (Apparently writing bad poetry doesn't make you "cool" in junior high school.) The worst part, well, other than the no-friend thing, was that the ringleader had been my supposed bestest friend in the group and the person to whom I told all my deep dark secrets . . . which she happily told to everyone as proof of her popularity worthiness.

two faces

HELEN DEVINE

a box, with sides
squares and corners
filled with a narrow mind
of all shapes and colors

don't pull off the ribbon
or undo the bow
or you'll see nothing fits in the right position
the current runs high over the feelings below

don't touch the box
it will make you bleed
don't buy into its cries of constant need
and if you still believe it's a gift of plenty
open the box, you'll find it empty

I wrote "Defect" in grade ten (1995). This was amidst my Hole/Veruca Salt/L7 phase where I thought old, nasty, secondhand dollies from the thrift store were the shit. I thought that if I could create something "deep" that was based on a metaphor involving such a cool fashion accessory, that I, too, would be the shit. I know it wasn't uncommon for the mid-'90s, but, I thought old, mutilated dolls were fashion accessories, as well as decorative ornaments. I had many of them arranged in suicide scenes around my bedroom; it looked like you were walking into a "Betsy Wetsy Goes to Hell" diorama. This poem was written about me not being able to fit in, thinking that there was something wrong with me, and that maybe if I could commit suicide I would be reincarnated as a normal girl. I thought that using dolls as examples of the normal kids was a brilliant metaphor to the plastic falsity of their personalities and lives. Yet at the same time, unlike a lot of kids, I thought that adults probably did know what they were talking about, and that I might regret killing myself, that the whole low self-esteem thing would be fine if I just waited it out. Good idea.

Defect

KIM SHAUGHNESSY

I'm a defected doll that needs to go back to the factory.
Thank you for playing with and humoring me when I wasn't like
    everyone
else's toys.
Right now I just want to go back to my factory.
But, I'm scared that maybe, being defective for so long may
    render me

impossible to remodel.

They might just melt me into a bottle.

Where there are no children playing with me.

Will they throw me out to rot?

Have I been recalled before?

Can I be remodelled more than once?

I wish I knew.

School—Poems About Cliques and Math Class

Part of being a teenager is finding out who your friends are and what **peer group** you want to belong to. Do you belong in the chess club, the drama club, the smoke pit, or the "cool group?" The **"cool group"** are the people that always have the hottest boy- or girlfriend, a nice car, good grades, and they are the people everyone wants to be **friends** with or to actually be. They may have made fun of the author or the author's friends, and poetry is one way of dealing with these **feelings**, whether they be of admiration, disgust, or hate.

Or—these poems could be about a suburban **gang** called the Flava that liked to drive around egging people, calling you "Dirty Girl." True Story.

I hated junior high when I was around thirteen or four-
teen because it was then that social groups seemed to
matter, and I really didn't fit in anywhere for those years.
Heck, I wore sweatpants for the first month of grade seven. I also
started to listen to too much Nine Inch Nails, Nirvana, and angry
music on the local university radio. And thus we have our angst
poem of not fitting in.

I

Z. K. TAYLOR

I'm too nice
I'm too mean
I'm a friend
What is a friend?
I'm not a lover
I'm not a mean person
I'm not a nice guy
Who am I?
Who am I?
What am I?
Why am I?
How am I?
Where am I?
You can tear out my heart
Smash it
Eat it
Burn it
Bury it

And it will still live
For it is made of stone
That softens once in a while
It stopped feeling long ago
I showed it reality
It understands now
I can kill
I can be kind
I can live
I can die
All at the same time
Why
Oh
Why
Oh
Why am I?

I was a good student in the ninth grade and as a consequence ended up doing all the hard math and science courses in high school. Of course, at that point I had already decided that I really didn't want a career in any of the sciences, but for some stupid reason (or rather a parental reason) I took honors math and science with the kids from the computer club, the chess club, the math club, and the pi memorizing club (yes that's right, pi memorizing as in $\pi = 3.141 \ldots$ whatever on to infinity). Needless to say my math and science marks were not ideal and I was in the normal courses with the normal kids by grade eleven.

Untitled

Z. K. TAYLOR

Ack!
I am sick of school
But I have to go
I want to be me
Not a scientist
Not a mathematician
So why do I
Do advanced science-math
Do they think we're
Machines that don't have
Lives. Do they think
We're having fun
Ahhh well fuck
That . . . . It's
Shit . . . . .

Got to keep going
Got to keep going
Got to keep going . . . . .
That Sucks

In jr. high school English class, we had an assignment to do a parody poem of "'Twas the Night Before Christmas." I decided to do it on this group of grade tens that called their group of friends, or gang, or posse—if you will: The Flava crew (pronounced Fley-va).

I swear to God they came up with that name themselves! Now, these boys were not really a gang. They were more like rich kids with too much time and testosterone on their hands. They would drive past us in the morning and yell out obscenities at my friend Sarah and me, like: "dirty girl," "dirty skid," "dirty punk," and variations there on.

The funny thing is, I think the Flava were scared of us. They didn't quite know what we were all about. I think they thought we had gang relations so even though they would egg us on with their words, they never actually followed through on their threats.

The Flava graduated from high school with mediocre grades and have grown up to pump my gas and work at their father's oil and gas companies. How's that for No Fear?

The Night Before High School

SARA BYNOE

'Twas the night before high school, when all through the home
Not a child was sleeping, not even Jerome;
His school clothes were hung in his closet on hooks,
And then on the floor were his backpack and books.

The children were petrified all cold in their beds,
While visions of eggings haunted their heads

I'd just had a bath and a nice facial wrap
And was settling down to have my cat nap,

When out on the lawn there arose a stew
I sprang from my bed to see the Flava crew.
Our suburban gang who likes to terrorize kids
Especially those of us they call "dirty skids."

The moon shone on this gang, illuminating their heads
And I thought this is it—we'll all soon be dead.
When, what to my wondering eyes should appear,
But a long black truck with a sticker—NO FEAR,

With a short little driver, so stupid and dumb,
And car full of beer cans and girls smacking gum.
More drunk than frat boys the posse they came,
And I stop realizing that I knew each of their names;

"There's Kempthorn, and Craig-o, and Matthew and Bob
And Morrison, and Graham, and Bradford and Rob.
To the top of Oakridge to the end of Braeside
Now go away, go away run and all hide!"

As spoiled brats that are used to getting their way
This wasn't what the Flava usually heard people say,
So to the porch front the posse stepped up.
And they gave me a look that made me shut up.

And then, in a twinkling, I heard on the street
The sirens and wheels of cops on the beat.

As I turned my head, to hear the cop's sound,
The Flava they egged me! and then fell to the ground.

I couldn't believe they had egged me
I thought they were out, down at their pit party.
They all got in their fancy cars screamed, "Yuck to you"
Then they all laughed—even the Flavettes, too.

So the cops chased them down Avenue 90
And driving away they were feeling pretty high and mighty—
    (but mostly high)
When the cops finally got them; the cops said, "Kids this ain't a
    joke"
And the Flava responded, "Hey man, wanna toke?"

The cop took the joint then declared, "Boys you've been tricked
that ain't marijuana that's a bag of catnip."
Craig-o said to Morrison, "I knew you weren't baked,
And his reply was, "Come on man, we've always faked."

Now the streets are all safe now that the Flava's behind bars
No more drinking Kokanee, no more stealing golf cars.
But I heard them exclaim as they were lead to their cells,
"You fucking niners can just go to Hell!
We're the Flava Crew!

In grade five I decided I didn't want to be a hunchback. Not that I was one already, and needed to remedy it, but that I never wanted to become one. So, everyday I was aware of my posture. I sat with a straight back and trained my young body to stand aligned and balanced. I held my head up like my dad told me I should. Then this bitch named Clare (also in grade five) came up behind me one day and said something about how tall and proud and straight I was sitting, something along the lines of, "Nice posture, geek," and I slouched down into my seat. In fact, I'm slouching right now. She blew my chance at never being a hunchback . . . but the worst part is, I let her. That was elementary school.

Apparently

POLLY DICTEZ

Apparently they speak of me when I'm not around
Call me "such a rebel,"
And then they let me down.
Apparently they wish I'd talk,
They don't know what I'd say
For if I spoke the thoughts I think,
I think they'd go away.
Apparently they seem to care,
About me a little bit,
Bite my tongue,
Lease my mind,
I'm sick of all their shit.

I was in grade seven going to a private school while
Jenny, my friend from elementary, went to public
school. I was the Goody Two-shoes while Jenny was the
epitome of "bad girl." She smoked, drank, and fooled around with
older guys. I dreamed that one day I'd be as cool as she, that one
day I'd fit in, if only for a moment.

Jenny and Me

JOLEEN SADLER

For she is the one who has the power
of all the trees and the flowers
but one of the flowers is starting to wilt
the one who wears a tie and a dead-ugly kilt

For she is the teased and cheated-on one
whenever there is a problem she starts to run
she is ugly and has no friends

For she is the one who needs to mend
the power that she actually really needs
is just to be liked by all the flowers and trees

Not best friends or friends at all
just to be liked for one day that's all

Holy shit, my first day of high school really, really sucked. It was a huge place, and I got horribly lost the second I walked into the doors. I was late for every class, because I just couldn't find the damn places. To make matters worse, of course, I was bound to bump into my ex-boyfriend (the subject of "You Also Suck") because he went to that school. But I didn't so much "bump into him" as I "bashed my own face into a locker." I saw him coming down the hall, and did a hasty about-face—right into an open metal locker door. Brilliant. It was so smooth. I may have looked like a complete dork, but hopefully he got the message: "I'd rather smack my own face into a slab of cold steel than talk to you." It took me awhile to learn to find my way around, and to learn to pretend the guy wasn't there, but I learned the first day to watch the hell out for open locker doors in crowded hallways.

I Hate High School

SARAH F.

Only one
Within two thousand
I get smaller
Claustrophobia!
I'm scared shittless
Too many people
I've lost myself
The building eats me
I'm nervous and edgy
I can hardly breathe

My heart feels squeezed
The surroundings know it
And feed on my fear
No way in hell I stand a chance in here

Like so many teen-angst poets, I had my very own bully who seemed completely dedicated to making other people's lives a misery, but especially mine. I tried everything to get him off my back; ignoring him, throwing insults or threats at him, complaining to the vice principal, kneeing him in the groin . . . if any of it worked, the effects didn't last, and the Jackass just wouldn't leave me alone. One day, I was hanging out with my buddy "Shitface," playing pool, when the Jackass's friends show up (without Jackass). Shitface said, "Hey, you should read them that poem . . ." I said, "No way, they'll kick my ass!" But he insisted. When I did, they stated cracking up and howling with laughter. They told me things like: "He can be a fuckin' jerk. . . . He's really messed up, we only let him hang out with us because we feel sorry for him." It validated my theory that he really was an asshole in everybody else's eyes, even his "friends!" I considered it my best poem EVER for at least two years after that. Oh, the things you consider brilliant at the time. . . .

Untitled (The Asshole Poem)
SARAH F.
Grade 9, age 14–15

You annoying stupid asshole
You disgusting putrid Fuck
In the lottery of brain cells
You hadn't any luck
You smirk with that annoying face
And show that stupid grin
And stick up high your empty head

Until I want to bash it in
You think you're something special
You think you're something great
But your parents used their birth control
About nine months too late
You have a massive ego
But you have a tiny brain
And the way that you think you're hot shit
Is driving me insane
Why you love yourself so much is really hard to see
And the reasons for your confidence
Remain a mystery
You're conceited and deluded
But one day you'll realize,
That you're nothing but an asshole
In everybody else's eyes

When I was in grade ten, I spent a ridiculous amount of time hanging out at the school's "smokepit," an area next to the tracks where the kids were allowed to go smoke. I didn't smoke (at least not *cigarettes*), but everybody I knew was always down there—all the time, and I do mean *all* the time. Most of us skipped an insane amount, and never got into huge trouble for it (unless you count being shoved into remedial classes or having to take summer school).

A lot of people in high school couldn't wait to "grow up," whatever that is. They couldn't wait to be "free," to be out on their own either to party all the time, or to make a pile of cash. (I wonder how that's working out, guys. . . .)

I was never one of those people. In high school, we had our bum in the butter, and I knew it. I had a parent to take care of me, and made a career of slacking. I wasn't that proud of being a useless git, hanging out with stoners all day, but I knew that the "Real World" was a scary, ruthless place, and I'd rather stay where I was. "Growing Up" is for suckers. All good things must come to an end, and I was getting nostalgic for it before it had even ended.

The Smokepit Poem

SARAH F.
Grade 10, age 15

We will chill
So we don't choke
We feel happy
Although we're broke
We sit out here

Where the sun will shine
And make the most of our passing time
When I'm out here among my friends
I wish this time would never end
And when high school's in the past
I'll remember this time as a blast
No rent, bills, jobs, or mundane shit
I'd rather be here in the pit
We lie and suntan on the track
It suits us fine that the rules are slack
No teachers come to kick our ass
And tell us to get back to class
The approaching future feels like "never"
And I wish that this could last forever.

This one had a title (and a very appropriate one, too!). I found it written on loose-leaf paper that was ripped out of a science notebook. I knew it was a science notebook because it had those little holes from those tight metal coil bindings. Judging by the other graffiti on the page, Sonic Youth's *Goo* album had just come out. I can deduce from this that it was written in grade eleven English class. I was seventeen. At this time I remember feeling like I had no brain. That I was completely useless. That there was nothing I was even remotely good at. As I grew up I realized you don't have to be good at anything, you just have to pretend to be. If you don't believe me, turn on the TV. (No don't bother. Just take my word for it.)

Why can't I

PAUL ANTHONY

Why can't I think? Why can't I read?
Why can't I talk? Why can't I concentrate?
Why can't I spell? Why can't I have an opinion?
Why can't I express it?
Why can't I write a poem?

Life Sucks and I Want to Die

As the category title implies, these are poems about wanting to **die**. The images in these poems are **dark** and bloody. This category is an extreme of the **I Am Alone** category because these poems are very **hopeless**. A lot of people in their teen years wrote poems about how much they **hate life,** and death, as they see it, is their only way to escape. Having lived through this phase, I can see that these poems are positive to share because they show that other people experience this feeling and that one does grow out of it. It should be noted that all authors of these poems are alive and happy today, and able to see some humor in their **cry** for help.

I wrote this poem in jr. high. At one point I enjoyed this poem so much, that I wrote it out in funky calligraphy and posted it on my wall right beside my bed; I don't know if that perpetuated my depression or if it encouraged my writing.

This is definitely a poem that was written on tear-stained paper.

What I Want to Do

SARA BYNOE

Bitter tears fill my eyes
fuzzed sight and then i cry
tears falling to my chin
tears that say i did not win
sour smile of quivering lips
hold it in and then i flip
hysteric heaves wanting breath
visioning thoughts questioning death
sweet relief of revenge and power
a new emotion for every hour
happy sad and now i'm through
what on earth am i to do
say its over say i'm done
saying things i have begun
start and never finish
things i want
things i wish
want more time to redo
what on earth am i to do?

Again . . . influenced by Jim Morrison . . . and the death wish . . . funny thing is . . . I was never that upset about things . . . I was never suicidal . . . I think I was just having a shitty day and felt like no one cared or understood me . . . nobody but Jim. {See the Fuck You category—"A Wish" for more on Michelle's Doors obsession}

Untitled

MICHELLE BJOLVERUD

I'm at the end of my rope
I can take no more
Cut the strings
Let me be free
I want to fly
I want to die

I want to see the sky
I want to see myself die

Just my body not my soul
It will live on in the hearts, minds,
and souls of others

If that happens, then I never really will die

I was a "head" with whom none of the heads would hang out. They didn't beat me up (that was left to the jocks) but they didn't acknowledge me either. (I didn't mind, I think, because they were pretty scary.) In retrospect, I suppose I was a nerd/head amalgam. I was also a fifteen-year-old, un-laid, frustrated, zit-poppin' dumbass. I suppose I wanted to get back at the world for making me into all of the above, and since I didn't have the orbs to literally off myself, I guessed that the next best thing would be to do it literally. In my twisted little mind, the more people read this poem, the more they would want to watch over me, to ensure that I didn't actually follow through. Ironically, when this stuff appears in print, I may be responsible for career suicide.

How I Killed Myself
HARICOT JONES

The keenness lent to wrong belief
I thought the blade was cutting deep
(The mind it plays to cause deception
Except in times of retrospection)
The blood a boring simple trickle
Down my neck around my nipple
Ever slower left my chest
Upon my belly stopped to rest
Life it did not pass my eyes
Or futures still unrealized
Only dreams of vacant trances
Soothing peace my brain enhances
The second time a little stronger

The path of scarlet ever longer
Around my feet accumulating
Standing smiling suffocating
Apparent look of shock I had
Once naked now in crimson clad
I closed my eyes to look around
Saw nothing and made no more sound.

"Bloody Murder, Separately We Will Die" was written when I was about fifteen, as an ode to my best friend, Sam. We had dated for about eight months in grade nine, had been best friends since grade eight, got back together in our grad year, and lived together until we were about twenty-one. We are actually still inseparable to this day, for the most part. Although, he now lives away in a cabin with his boyfriend, and I live on Commercial Drive in Vancouver with my girlfriend, we still have a pretty irreplaceable friendship. In retrospect, we were the Queer As Folk answer to Kurt Cobain and Courtney Love. The reason I wrote this poem was because I was mad that regardless of any other boyfriends I tried to have during high school, I couldn't ever really meet anyone I connected with like I did with him. Yet, at the same time, if we dated, we tore each other to shreds with bitchscraps everyday (maybe it's cuz we were both gay?), so I was pretty much screwed. No boys would go out with me because I always seemed to be preoccupied with affection for him (at least that's the reason I'd like to remember), so I wanted him dead. Then I guess I thought that if I killed him, I'd still have to live with the memory that I killed him, and I'd never be rid of him, so, of course, the most reasonable outcome would be for us to both die. My early teen obsession with gore, however, is inexplicable.

Bloody Murder, Seperately We Will Die

KIM SHAUGHNESSY

I want to kill you.
With my bare hands.
I want your blood on my hands.

In my hair.
On my clothes.
In my mouth.
In my veins.
I will live off of your life's blood until I die.
Oh yes, you will die.

I want it gone.
Your blood's in my veins.
Get it out.
Rip it from me.
Bleed myself dry.
Just to be without you.
Stab it out.
Squeezing and scraping every last drop out of me.
Oh yes, I will die.

I want it pure.
Our blood united.
Clean from us and our sins.
Together it gives life.
Together it takes life.
My blood killed you.
Your blood killed me.
Bloody murder we are dead.
Bloody murder, we are separately dead.
Oh yes, we will die.

I wrote this after jealousy destroyed a very dear friendship. Things were said and done that couldn't be erased by anything other than time. At the time it all felt hopeless. I thought the only thing that I could do to get this friend to love me again would be to die. But death was not an apology I was willing to offer. And in living I felt that I had no pulse, no life, no feelings because I couldn't offer the apology that I knew was warranted.

Now I think about the hopelessness that I felt then and think about the whole situation. Time has erased all that happened and the friendship has been repaired to a degree. This little mishap is never discussed but mutually remembered for all its pettiness. I know from other failed friendships that you can only apologize so much for things you have said or done. But the only thing that repairs a friendship is time and acceptance. You have to accept your friends' flaws and your own flaws, and be humble enough to forgive so that you might someday be forgiven.

Untitled

GAYLE BURKHOLDER

If I were to give you my pulse
Would you trust me once more?
I would give you my pulse if it would help
But my pride would just get in the way.
My pulse is so hidden from me now
Maybe I'm just incapable of remaining.
How many times can one miss saying, "I'm sorry?"

This is an ode to being a prisoner of love in yet another unhappy relationship. It was a damned if you leave, damned if you stay kind of situation. I was so in love with this boy, but we were on two different planes that were farther apart than Venus and Mars. He never did understand the ways of my mind, and I used to like to delude myself into thinking that one day he would. This poem was written on one particularly depressing day when the delusion no longer wanted to hold itself up and I was thinking about the alternative solution to the damned if you leave, damned if you stay situation. The easiest escape is the eternal sleep, and if you glorify it with visions of angels, and peace, and a glorious afterlife, which I like to refer to as home, it doesn't seem half bad. Does it? Especially when you are feeling miserable and everything sucks.

RELEASE ME

GABRIELLA KRISS

All I am is in me,
All I am aches to be free,
All that I am seeking,
Is balance and release,
Pain is my addiction,
Love is my disease.

I crave for my soul mate,
To kill the silence,
To shelter each other from the rain,
To feel each other's deepest pain.

Tell me again, how beautiful death is,
Tell me again, there is nothing I will miss,
Summon my dark angel,
To bring me his kiss,
Lend me peace,
And release all this.

Fuck You—You Don't Understand Me!

These are poems full of **anger** and **frustration**. Writing these poems was an outlet for feelings that the author deemed inappropriate to express in any other way. Perhaps in writing, **"fuck you"** poems the author is allowed the freedom of revenge or venting without facing the repercussions that their desires will cause. Most often, they use a lot of capital letters, exclamation points, and **curse words**.

This angst came about because of a week where I did not do anything wrong and still had the whole "world" on my case. What am I talking about? I make it to all my classes and my teachers tell me I'm not trying hard enough. My report card was honor roll material and my parents are on me for not being one of the top students. Even my friends were on me for working part-time.

What "created" the poem was on the Saturday of that week, I had the door closed to my room and my mom asked me what I was doing. I can't remember the tone she used, but I went ballistic. I was yelling and screaming to be left alone. I don't know how long my rant went, but I remember the best line. "I'm planning nuclear doom." It kind of lost something in the translation.

The thing I find funny about this poem is how extreme it is over how petty and small the "incidents" were. I guess it shows how magnified life is when one is a teenager.

Fuck, What Now?

ROEHL

Fuck you and you and you and you.
Oh yeah, and fuck me, yeah, fuck me, too.

I am tired of playing kiss-ass games,
where I'm just a number, please no names.

When did being a kid become so tough,
just because your parents say they had it rough.

Fuckin' Monty Python had it right,
when they sent that cow out of sight.

Because when life just sucks, I want to die,
I want to take off and fly in the sky.

Fuck, what now? Keep out of my room,
I'm fucking plotting the fucking world's doom.

 The scary part in writing about the "inspiration" for this poem is that I can still remember the events that led to the angst that came out in the poem. What is scarier is I laugh as hard as the audience when I read this one at a Teen Angst Poetry reading. I don't know what that says about me.

My best friend in grade ten was a girl and to protect the innocent I won't give her name. Some people might think that at that age wanting her as a girlfriend had to be part of the friendship, but it was really one of those buddy-type relationships. I was also a good friend of Nick. She was infatuated with Nick. It was "Nick smiled at me today," "Do you think Nick likes me?," etc., for at least a month. Until it was "Nick asked me out on a date!," "I had a great time with Nick." and "Nick is such a great guy." The rough part for me was that I knew Nick was dating other girls while this infatuation was going on. I tried to hint about Nick's activities, but she was completely oblivious. I got so tired of hearing how wonderful Nick was (when I knew he was two/three-timing) that I told her that I was sick of hearing about Nick. (Hence the poem.) We ended up not talking for a couple of weeks. She came crying to me when she found out about the other girls. I have to admit that I wasn't mature enough at that time to be empathetic and our friendship wasn't the same after that.

Sick of Nick

ROEHL

If I hear, Nick, Nick, Nick,
one more time I will be sick.

We are just friends now, I understand,
but things are getting out of hand.

Girl, you don't know when you're being used,
because you keep saying he's just confused.

Well I've lost count of the times you've cried,
or told me you'd just wished you'd died.

Well as a friend, I just have to say,
I'm sick of Nick, at least for today.

 Basically I listened to the Doors a lot while I was in junior high and high school. I idolized Jim Morrison. I read all the books about the Doors and Jim and continued on to read books that had influenced him. Jim sang about life, death, and everything in between and he didn't seem to care what anyone else thought. At that point in my life I totally related and my poems represent a voice that couldn't figure out how to express itself in a positive manner or even figure out what it was trying to say. Looking back I'm not sure what I was sooooo angry about but I think it all has to do with a girl who didn't want to (or maybe was too scared to) own up to her thoughts and feelings so she wrote in an abstract form without using the word "I" to identify herself as the subject.

"A Wish" is definitely stolen or should I say borrowed from the long live version of the Doors song "The End." Listen to the song and you'll understand.

A Wish

MICHELLE BJOLVERUD

Have you ever wanted them all dead?
For death just to invade their
soul and take over

I have
and I will again

If I had any spare change that's what I would do

Ha Ha Ha Ha Ha
Kill the mother
Kill the father
Kill him
Kill him

DESTROY US ALL!!!!!!!!!!!!!!!!
(we need not deserve to live)

 I was seventeen, and Acutane had miraculously smoothed out my pizza face (not to mention my pizza back and chest. Mmmm . . . pizza.) Self-confidence was a recent discovery to me, and I was using it to all advantage. Women were around me always, talking to me, massaging my shoulders, meeting me at my locker, walking ME to class. I was juggling them, flipping them like burgers. Everything was fantastic. Until she came along. A ferocious beauty named Jen, smarter than me and willing to prove it. She beat me at my own game. Now I was the fast food, and she was flipping me. When I found out how many others she had on the go, I flipped out, right off that grill. But I was already burned. (Sorry about the ham-handed analogy.) Of revenge this poem speaks, of hatred as pure as vodka. Of testosterone gone awry.

Fuck You

HARICOT JONES

Don't come to me
To cure your itch
You beef-witted rancid
Whorebag bitch
'Cause if you do
I'll dig a ditch
And throw your runty
Garbage ass in it!
FUCK YOU!
FUCK YOU!
May gophers gnaw on your tits

And spiders crawl up your ass
I'd rather have some fun
On this side of my gun
And watch them sew
Your arms back on again
YEE HAW!

 I seemed to have a bad habit throughout my teens of winding up sitting beside creeps (on buses, in my driver's ed. course, in other classes). This particular creep was in a class, and therefore harder to shake than usual, especially since I'd been friendly at first. It was extra irritating since I was, as usual, pining for a lost ally, and the contrast was increasingly intolerable. His creepiness was kind of scary, too, but all it took in the end was a little hostility to fend him off, so in retrospect the poem's a little unnecessarily harsh.

Untitled

JAN KRISTY

I'll never take a Hershey's kiss from you
And don't you dare do anything again
that reminds me of my friend
because you're not worthy of that comparison
Your nature is stunted and warped
and it scares me to death
Don't you dare picture me
or hold my face even in your head
I won't be a character in the
twisted theater of your mind
Don't even speak my name
How dare you presume to ask
how my weekend was?
I don't want to know how yours was.
I don't want to know anything about you,
don't want to remember your face,

your voice, your name—
those souvenirs that should only pass
and be kept between friends—
I refuse to remember you.
I hate the indignity of your cigarette breath,
and I hate the confessions you pour on me
that I don't want to hear
Your liking scares me
Your jealousy terrifies me
How dare you replace my sweet dreams
and fond memories
with the nightmare that is you?

 I wrote this poem while having a "fight" with my best friend. Of course, I do not remember the details as to why we were fighting, but I know that I have always been a nonconfrontational sort of gal. And, that is why I would turn to my writing and let it all out because no one really understood my pain.

The problem with being alone and no one understanding your pain is that it leads to a lot of bottled-up emotions. It is in poems like this that some of that anger against the world comes out Now wouldn't the world be better if we could vent our anger through poetry rather than violence? I think so. However, I know that I still have tendencies to bottle up my "fuck offs"—as I am sure most people do. Hmmm? Maybe we should all say "fuck off" more often? Ah, but then I would probably have no friends because there are lots of times I stop my expletives on friends, and ignore the problem. Maybe I should rephrase the "fuck off" into something more acceptable like . . . like . . . I cannot think of anything else. Because when I want to say fuck off, that is all I want to say. See, teen angst continues to this day.

October 30, 1996
SARA BYNOE

I wish I could tell you how much I hate you
How much I despise laughing at your jokes
I dislike being in your presence
You make me feel creepy and bad
When my mind is saying "fuck off" and
The words that come out are "that's nice"

I realize I may never be able to fully express my emotions.
I have all this hate inside repressed
Because I don't want you to hate me
Why do I care?
I don't know
I want to yell and scream
But instead I work the problem out
Someday I'm gonna burst
I pity the person that is around at that moment
FUCK YOU!

 There's almost no doubt in my mind that I wrote this poem minutes after the subject left. In fact, I may have even started composing it in my head while he was buttoning his fly or making awkward, thanks-for-the-blowjob-gotta-run conversation as he tied up his Vans.

We started out childhood best friends. I know, isn't that always the way? But, as the years passed, I guess we discovered we had more in common than preferring My Little Pony over He-Man. If memory serves, the fateful night was in August the year we were to enter grade six. We were camped out in sleeping bags in his back-yard and could clearly see his mother making cookies in the kitchen while I reached over and gave Joey a handjob. Looking back, I should've volunteered to help his mom, but what did I know?

For better or worse, we soon fit the definition of "best friends with benefits." We still hung out and did all the stuff we always did, but we also saved time for a good romp before going home. By high school, sex was the only thing keeping our friendship together, and just barely. The transaction between our bodies had become quite ordered and efficient: He called, he came over, we did it, he left. On nights when he was lazy or couldn't borrow his parent's car, we did it over the phone, my geography homework momentarily thrown to the side.

Call me romantic, but I soon wanted more than getting off with a guy who spent longer getting to my house than he ever did inside. It was around the same time that a woman in the United States reportedly severed her husband's penis because he was abu-sive and demanding in bed. While I had trouble condoning her ac-tions, at the very least, I had to admit that part of me was envious of her spunk.

Joe

MATT PEARSON
Sept. 28, 1995
Age 17

will anyone buy this two-dollar acid trip?
i could have sworn you just said you loved me
do you know what love is?

you whip it out and cram it down my throat
it's time like these that i wish i knew
Lorena Bobbit personally

with your Gap clothes and your big friends
you flutter around from circle to circle
like a bee collecting nectar in a flowerbed

i see through your soul like it's a
freshly polished window
the aura of your personality is about as thick as
the smoke that rises from one single match

you are nothing to me
stay far away

next time
i might bite

Political Action— Fight the Power

For a teenager the world is an oyster where life is full of possibilities. Teenagers are the **future** and these poems were written by teens who wanted to make a **positive impact** on the world. Some of these poems were assignments from school; some were inspired by the **insane world** around them. The topics here range from **war**, to **vegetarianism**, conformity, and others.

This would be a Fight the Power poem. At a time when boys are becoming awkward men. A time when you'd agree with the statement, "It's the little things that kill." Perhaps letting my mother know in a subtle way that her generation was backward and I'm just setting things straight.

"The Eyes of My Youth Are Critical Ones."

G. MICHAEL GRAY

1997

If a pen marks itself on the inside of the pocket of your shirt,
it seems not to be a problem,
yet, if a pen swipes across the front of your shirt it becomes
a dirty shirt . . . and requires a wash.
We need to destroy that notion!
Work from the inside out.
I want to wash my shirt every time
I get ink on the inside,
and ignore the scar every time a dagger swipes across my chest.

If only an advertising genius could have tapped into the marketing supercomputer known as my brain at the age of fourteen. This poem has its own catchy byline (but no title): "Pollution hurts so please stop it. It's now or never." If only they would have sent someone to me instead of Justin Trousersnakes for that McDonald's commercial but alas my talent has been wasted. . . .

Untitled--Pollution Kills Acrostic

HEATHER TAYLOR

Please help our world, the
Ozone, so we can
Live to see another day only to
Use more of our world up
Taking the lives of many
Including ourselves
Until
One day we won't remember why we are
Now dead or being
Killed or
Ill, praying to a
Lord who cannot help us anymore but
Little do we know that we will be
Sick forever.

I think I wrote this one in my biology 20 class . . . some days it was just sooooo boring. But using large words like "copulations"—definitely reflective of Jim Morrison's poetry and songs. (see A Wish—Fuck You category)

Untitled

MICHELLE BJOLVERUD

A world of boredom Invading our hearts
Black lungs
Rotting tongues
Reaching for something that does not exist (why do we exist?)

Peaceful copulations
with a vengeance in their souls

War is coming and it won't be pretty

I wrote this rap song when I was thirteen. I had dreams of being in a rap band. I was called "Boywonder," which I got shaved in the back of my head. DJ D.J.B. (Dion James Borley) when he was on the mic, was called "MC White" (a play on the artist "MC Lite"). Our Philipino friend Jon sometimes joined our fake band as our "Brown skin brother" aka MC "Lightly toasted." See, I grew up in suburban Winnipeg, there was only one black kid in our elementary school and he was a couple years older. His name was Gaylord Gasmen. The only black kid and his parents had to name him Gaylord?! I guess it meant something different in Trinidad. I heard years later when he gradu- ated college he changed his name. Too bad. I always loved that name.

Black & White Must Unite (Stop the Violence)

PAUL ANTHONY

One Friday night me boys gone chillin' at the mall, when some
    bully black man punched my homeboy D.J.B. for no reason
    at all.
He had a chain, no brain, the man was insane, you could tell he
    was game.
"Want to step out side," he said with a glare in his eye. "Why,"
    my D.J. replied, don't want no sucker die
Black and White, must unite (Stop the violence)
Black and White, must unite (Stop the violence)
Black and White, must unite (Stop the violence)

Do you read me, please comprehend, friend, before it's the end,
maybe now we could mend, 'cuz . . .

Black and White, must unite (Stop the violence)

Black and White, must unite (Stop the violence)

Black and White, must unite (Stop the violence)

Another time us guys were at a club, our friend Vince (cause he
had a car) purposely came very close to a black he'd rub.

Brain cells he lack, his knack is hack, another unprovoked at-
tack. "Oops, I missed," he said as he hissed, you get the gist,
the black boy be pissed, in the air shook his fist. Ya see need-
less to say that friend Vince, we haven't talked to him since.

Black and White, must unite (Stop the violence)

Black and White, must unite (Stop the violence)

Black and White, must unite (Stop the violence)

Racism hurts everyone, that's no fun, lets be done, put down
that gun, 'cuz . . .

Black and White, must unite (Stop the violence)

Black and White, must unite (Stop the violence)

Black and White, must unite (Stop the violence)

(Together we'll be much stronger)

Black and White, must unite (Stop the VIOLENCE!)

((music stops))

We're just killing ourselves.

This poem was written about the same time I became a vegetarian. It was very hip at that time in the all-ages punk rock scene to be a vegetarian or a vegan. My boyfriend and my best friend were vegetarians and were experimenting with veganism. I had cut back red meat, and was only eating chicken some of the time. But since both of my closest friends were vegans I figured I *had* to go vegetarian. It wasn't just peer pressure, I agreed with the politics behind it, and the health reasons.

Then I watched a film that showed a cow being slaughtered. After that, I knew I could never eat another living thing. I had always been an advocate for animal rights. I was against animal testing, using animals for entertainment, and I was against fur; the next logical step was to stop eating them too.

I am embarrassed to say that I am actually quite proud of this poem—well not the poem itself. It is a bit preachy, but I am proud that I have stuck to my morals and that I was a teenager who wanted to change the world not just one that passively accepted it. Besides, I'm sure I would have eventually become a vegetarian without my friends anyway—right?

Not Our Species

SARA BYNOE

Taped mouths, screaming with pain
Suffering so greatly
Without a hope of protecting themselves
Caged, beaten, tested and scared
Silent victims of our inventions

Without choice
Without a voice
They feel, they hurt, they cry
Turning every cheek they persevere
It's our fault it continues
Without the power to aid themselves
Without energy to bite the hand that hits
It's up to us
To love, to help, to solve, to rescue
Pain is unnecessary
Love is unconditional
It may be inconvenient
But so is suffering

This was one of many "This world is so cruel and evil" poems—you know, deep shit, like about how evil consumerism is, but how I'm one of the few brave souls who saw through it. I became a vegan, and my family started calling me "Lisa Simpson" and "Joan of Arc," and I just went off and wrote more of this. I refused to wear new clothes, spent way too long living almost exclusively on soy milk, apples, and Mr. Noodles, and started using the word "feedlot" way too much. I thought this would sound good as the lyrics to a Hardcore song.

Streamlined Feedlot Filters

SARAH F.

Streamlined Feedlot Filters
Assimilation of a nation
Glitter covered garbage
Distraction for the malcontent
Everything in life's a choice
Scream all you want and lose your voice
Trinkets of deceit
Keep our "sanity" intact
Blinkers for the people
Destiny engraved in stone
Strong souls must swim
Against the tide
No way for you to live outside
Your path's laid out before you
But you must find your way alone.

I cannot remember exactly what inspired this poem, but it is interesting to note that the notebook I found it in is a Ziggy journal that is stained with an odd red substance. However I am sure that at the moment I wrote this poem I thought I was being unbelievably profound. That no one had ever thought these thoughts before! I was breaking new ground—a radical punk rock girl in grade seven. What is the point to jog? We're going to die anyway . . . and why can't I say "fuck," "shit," "bitch" if they are only words?

I knew I was fighting against something I just didn't know what yet, so I let the rhyming scheme take over (and I really liked chorus' as well—can you tell?).

Why

JOLEEN SADLER
Aug 6–7 1995 (It took two days to write)

There are people in this world who just can't take
the way it's turning,
For God's Sake
See the surprise
People are high
Everyone lies
People die
We do fly
Ask why
or say goodbye
There are words in the language which no one can say
If they were so bad why were they made anyway

leave us be
we can speak free
don't you see
we don't drink tea
we are not what you want us to be
If a person chooses to die with a knife
Why would we save him
It's his choice of life
Is our sight fog
what's the point to jog
our trees turn to logs
were we once like the dog?
Everyone wants to know why we are here
We don't know because of our fear
fear that everything around us will change
That is why we are keeping in a certain range
Open your eyes
See the surprise
People are high
Everyone lies
People die
We do fly
Ask why
or say goodbye

Pointless Ramblings

Poems Made Up of Words That the Author Thought Sounded "Good" Together

These are very horrible poems, literarily speaking. There is no inspirational backstory behind them. The imagery often does not make any sense. Even the author does not know what the poem is about. These poems were written because the author liked the way the words sounded together or possibly because an image in the poem caused the author to riff on repetition of that theme. These were most often written in jr. high school before the author had much angst to write poems about.

"Random Findings" wasn't actually titled when I went through my old writing books to find stuff to submit to this anthology, so I tried to avoid any pretentious old habits and just name it after how I wrote it. It was written as part of a Creative Writing 11 exercise, which was to wander around the high school, finding random phrases and quotes and piece them into a work of literary art. This poem itself isn't that awful, but the poems I wrote after discovering this new writing method were a serious embarrassment. Unfortunately, I couldn't find them anywhere. What I started doing was making up "random phrases and quotes" that I thought were cool, morbid murder/death/destruction kinda stuff, piecing them together, then passing them off as a brilliant discovery that only someone as dark and gifted as myself could stumble upon. I think the impression I was trying to make with those other pieces to follow was that my life was just so cool, that I couldn't help but being surrounded by disturbing content to rip off on a constant basis.

Random Findings

KIM SHAUGHNESSY

See.
The stone.
Skip home.
You crazy earthlings are all alike.
Visitors welcome, please register at the office, thank you.
Help me, what do I do? Confused.
Machine profits support student activities.
Those who've got it, get it.

Looks good on you.

The maximum occupant load for these premises.

Stand back twenty feet, away from fire.

There was only one.

Mom and Dad were out, so we just got carried away.

Why search for the past?

The cause of the crash.

Because this poem is such a pointless-ramblings poem, the best way for me to explain it is to do a nearly line-by-line analysis of it. Here goes:

Grade nine was a horrible year. I was just recovering from total rejection from the cool group. I was making my own group of friends with the art freaks. That's why 9 is the number I lost my groove.

Blondie could be either my first boyfriend who had really blond hair or it could be the singer, I am not sure which it is.

I cannot remember what black roses stands for, but the "no shoes" line is a rip-off of the Beatles. My best friend at the time was a huge Beatles fan, so I guess some of it rubbed off.

Now the dog and cat analogy is back to the top of the poem—being left out of the cool group. I am a dog, as well as my friend Tanis (I'm not sure why we are dogs though), and the cat is the new popular girl. Tanis and the new girl became friends and left me out.

Melon = Blind Melon. My favorite band. They spoke to me in ways I thought no one could, and I was so in love with the acoustic guitarist.

Devils refers to my friend Jenny who was dating much older men.

I thought this last line was brilliant. And admittedly, to this day, I think that it is not that bad, for what I was trying to say at the time.

Christmas

JOLEEN SADLER

Things will get better, I know they will
Everything is adding up until
Everything is ahead of me until I move

9 is the number I lost my groove
SDRR (sex, drugs, rock and roll) are the words Blondie said
Somehow one of those will be the bed
The bed of black roses and walking across streets with no shoes
Fame then death is the worst thing you could lose
Two dogs were beside each other and a cat came to fame
with one of the dogs the cat's not to blame
either is the dog, they left one dog behind
made other friends, now the dog is still on the rind
People think in the past but they don't go to tell them
These are the words I learned from the melon
If you stop dreaming its time to die
I want to go where the world has eyes
Of many colors and marmalade skies
I've got to get there before I die
I'm not afraid to go to hell
I know what its like, someone told me well
I know many devils who are bold
All they are, are their parents who are trying to act old
They are playing house but they know it's not there
Acting cool pretending not to care
But really all they are, are kids who lose
being boosted up by their moms' high heel shoes

This is by far, the worst thing I ever wrote and shared with others. This poem was written in jr. high, when my friend Sarah and I were trying to be rock stars.

Yes, rock stars. We were going to have a band and it was going to be great. We spent a lot of time working on song lyrics and art direction for our albums, we also spent a lot of time thinking up clever band names. One of the names we came up with for ourselves was "The Best Band in the World." We thought it was a fun name because when people came to see us they could say, "I saw The Best Band in the World and man, did they ever suck." Maybe if we actually spent our time learning instruments instead of thinking up funny band names we might have gone somewhere. But with lyrics like "I wanna write a song" I don't think our chances were really good.

I Wanna Write a Song

SARA BYNOE

My emotions I wanna express
tell them as fast as Federal Express
how do you make it clear
make you feel like you are near
I wanna write a song
I wanna hear the gong of people
understandin' my feeling
I wanna write a song
I can't write
why do I bother?
I bother cause I wanna write a song

I wrote about Kong
I wrote about Vietnam
I wanna write a good song
I have tried and tried
I'm wasted no more inspiration
I tried to write a song
Could not hear the gong
I tried to write a song
It was bad

I don't recall having written this one, although the handwriting was unmistakably my own. I think I may have been on acid, or perhaps just shitfaced. Captain Morgan white was my drink in those days. The mickey size was in a plastic bottle, designed for fall-on-your-ass-drunken-fools like myself. I'd chase each swig with a sip of coke. I was so cool. But acid is a likelier culprit, as I just seemed to lose my train of thought. I never lost my train drunk. Drunk I was a loudmouth, unrelenting until the point was made, until the battle won. On acid, calm, stupid, kind, kenning with the universe, at one with the energy of the stupid masses. And thinking that all this stupid shit was actually really deep and intelligent. Mind swimming with "Whys" and "Hows," brimming with useless quandary, suffocating in the all encompassing "WOW" of the moment. Now that's a drug I could lose track on, and most certainly did many times. The question is, was this one of them? Maybe I was just really high on hash.

PEEYOU!

HARICOT JONES

My heart is ice
You are fire
Melt me with
Your thick desire
Watch my organ dissipate
Evaporate
Must be something that I ate
THIS IS A PIECE OF SHIT
ON THIS POEM I SHALL SPIT!

Rub it in watch the page wilt
This is a sad poem to have built
Forgive me, Lord, for being cheesy
But George will always love his Weasie.

When I was in Grade twelve, a friend and I drove to Barrie, Ontario, where we—along with another friend—rented a room at the Huronia Motel. I think it cost $46. We paid in cash. As we were leaving the small office, the man behind the desk pulled the cigarette from his mouth long enough to tell us he didn't want any "funny business." Which was odd, considering every other room at the joint seemed to be occupied by people with dubious intentions for the night.

It wasn't long after settling into our room that we decided to get down to business and do what we had come to do: chew about seven grams of magic mushrooms between the three of us. Why else would teenagers pay cash for a motel room?

Half an hour after chasing the mushrooms with bottles of lemon Fruitopia (not an advisable choice), we decided to go for a walk along the shore of Kempenfelt Bay. Somewhere along that shore, while Alex and Tessa sunk into their own trips, these poems were born One quite literally as I jabbered it at the time and transcribed it as best I could when we returned to the room, and the other, months later, after I had given the experience further thought.

I remember vaguely the white duck and three wise men from "something so right." The same poem is infused with much of the night's misguided intensity, yet it's also flavored by some of my wider influences at the time, namely Tori Amos. Who more would appreciate such a thing as, "immersed in thoughts of lemon drops and honey suckle"?

The sad thing is I thought these poems revealed my brilliance as both a writer and thinker. I thought they were my *Sgt. Pepper's Lonely Hearts Club Band* or *In Utero*. I thought I was destined to become the drugged-out writer of my generation, scrawling all of our hopes and dreams on napkins and scrap pieces of paper I found on the ground.

Instead, I was a seventeen-year-old kid, stoned out of my skull
with a couple of friends inside a shitty motel room far from home.

something so right

MATT PEARSON
May 29, 1996
Age 18

take me away and let us escape together
brought to this place by destiny and the need to flee from the
detrimental dictators guiding our young lives
our escape is a motel; a roadside dive; an oasis from the world of
    indifference
these orange walls have witnessed many things, but nothing as
    strange as
the exorcism of our own demons, yielding mirrors which reflect
    the picture of
the person we don't want to face:

ourselves.

immersed in thoughts of lemon drops and honey suckle,
i am intoxicated by your companionship
our souls are connected through some sort of
Divine Intervention
a connection that seems never-ending
a connection that provides stability in a world of unsteady
i am lost in all that is you, you have found yourself in all
    that is me

we remain side by side like the pieces of a jigsaw puzzle
we remain united in bliss
we remain children of fate
we remain linked for eternity and beyond

OranGe rOOm

MATT PEARSON
April 28, 1997
Age 18

velvet altar teasing the clouds
velvet Jesus,
smiling,
chilling on a popsicle-stick cross

dancing
jumping
laughing
singing
sinning

why did the lily-white duck float away into the charcoal night?
why did the three wise men forget to take us to the promised land?
why can't we see that star?

STAR

the one that gives guidance
                    hope
                    forgiveness

Odes—To Famous People
That Felt Your Pain
Like Kurt Cobain

These are poems for the **heroes** and the **icons** in a teenager's life. For the generation of current **twenty-somethings** that person was Kurt Cobain. Cobain was the leader of the grunge rock band Nirvana who **shocked** the world by "committing suicide" in 1994. Cobain's death came as a huge shock for all the **angst-filled** teenagers of the early 1990s. He lived the dream that they all had; of a person true to themselves, following a dream and being successful because of it. With Cobain's passing, fans wrote poems to understand the event, themselves, and the implications of a world without a hero. The other **ode poem** that is included in this section is an ode to hockey—another God for some.

I am thirteen years old. I have discovered myself through music. Life is good. I bought *In Utero* a few months ago. I go away to Vancouver Island for spring break to see my stupid family. I am mad. I should be at home with friends. I get on the ferry and there is some cryptic news about Kurt Cobain. What? He's not well? What happened? Was it another coma like in Rome?

I spend the next few hours on the ferry back to Vancouver in agony. What is happening in the world? I pray for my new Idol: Dear God let him be well. I get to Vancouver, turn on the radio: "Kurt Cobain was found dead in his Seattle home, due to a gun shot to the head. Kurt Cobain has killed himself." Noooooooo!!! I softly sob to myself in the car.

How can people go on with their lives knowing what has happened?! I get to my Aunt and Uncle's house in Vancouver; my uncle comes home and says: "Did ya hear? Kurt Cobain blew his brains out." Scoff. How could he joke about this? I spend the next few days watching Much Music listening for clues, insights, and reasons into this mysterious catastrophe. I listen to Courtney Love read his suicide note. Peace, Love, Empathy—whatever. Why? God why did this have to happen?

As you can tell I am still dealing with this sad loss to music history.

To Kurt Cobain

SARA BYNOE
April 12, 1994

Why Suicide?
Someone else should have died

Did you think ahead?
Did you know the impacts of your being dead?
You're selfish and dead
because you put a bullet to your head
In our hearts you will remain
But my feelings for you will never be the same
Our questions unanswered
The answers are gone
Never to be asked
Never to understand
Uncomprehendible note you left behind
You said you loved us—how so?
It's a shame—a rotten shame
It's done and over
Move on—Show's over
Peace, Love, Empathy?
Whatever.

I'm sitting in a smoke-filled bar in Mississippi, the big-screen TV is tuned to CNN and there are bottles of Michelob Light lined up along the bar in front of my dad. I'm thirteen years old, a new recruit to grunge, a resident of Seattle (in my dreams!), and a HUGE fan of Kurt Cobain. This is a long time ago now: when my dad still lived in Mississippi, when I still wore a green-and-black striped T-shirt, and when music still meant something . . . yup, a long, long time ago. . . .

He's dead! Kurt Cobain has killed himself! I look around the room and blame everyone there for never caring about him or understanding him. I blame CNN for WANTING to run a story like this since he first made it big. When we get back to our apartment, I sit in my air-conditioned bedroom and write this poem. I try to cry, but I can't. It's all just too profound.

Kurt

POLLY DICTEZ
April 27, 1994

He killed himself like he always knew he would,
Sunk his teeth into the bullet and let the pieces fly.
Left a broken heart of millions in the place where he once stood.
Music that could make you think,
Now I'm asking why.
He left us,
To be alone,
He left us,
To leave his own,
Killed a legend,

To make us cry,
Killed himself
So he could die.
Understanding, understood,
Underrated—not all good,
Overachiever of the underworld,
Now he is gone.

Being a hockey fan may seem inconsistent with maintaining the angsty teen persona, but my friends and I managed to reconcile the two. (In fact, we called our attempted band Offside (oooh, the symbolism)). Besides, I was a Hartford Whalers fan, which lent itself well to angst and despair.

Hockey fanship inevitably (for us) meant lots of terrible odes and other poetry. One "ode" began, thoughtfully:

Sometimes I want to take you home
And hang you on my wall;
But then I think, it wouldn't work,
They don't make frames that tall . . .

One of my friends, meanwhile, wrote the sensitively titled ballad "Boy We Hartford Whalers Really Suck" for me. It began:

Sometimes when I look up,
I have to think,
Where are the people surrounding our rink?
Maybe this is practice,
I must be wrong,
But the opera guy's singin' that anthem song . . .

This was also the era of the ninth-grade poetry wars. For English class that year we all had to write a series of poems of different types, and then take turns reading them aloud. We (a substantial part of the class) starting using this forum as a chance to continue our hockey arguments, and in fact would considerately give each other copies of our masterpieces. I remember receiving one with the classic line "Nick Kypreos will never tussle/Because he has no muscle." In retaliation for that particular one, I wrote a sonnet in perfect iambic pentameter insulting the writer's favourite team. (As well, Kypreos went on to win the Stanley Cup/though no longer with the Whalers/on my sixteenth birthday, against the Canucks. Ha!)

Anyway, my hockey fan career led me to be a program-seller for a local junior team one season. I wrote "Tribute" after the team's farewell dinner, and later even put it to weepy piano music, for Offside. (My friend, who bravely sang it, always insisted I should write music for long-distance telephone company commercials.)

Tribute or Season's End

JAN KRISTY

And now it's dark,
and now it's done
I didn't lose so
I guess I won
Farewell, farewell,
perfect, complete
I cried inside
but the tears were sweet
All such things
must have an end . . .
Why do I feel like I've lost
an old and dear friend?
I liked to think
you were really mine

Could take your hands,
sing "Auld Lang Syne"
But old acquaintance
must be forgot
This was the final lesson
you taught me
I wish you joy
and dreams come true
And may the world
always smile on you
You're my silver cup,
now it's filled right up
You're my flag
and I'll always lift it up
I hope you find a hold
in some heart of gold
But no one, no one,
will ever take your place to me.

For Fun—Silly Poems About Silly Things

Teenagers are not just depressed and angsty, they also like to **laugh** and sometimes it's at themselves. For **Fun** poems capture this feeling. Some of these poems were meant to be **songs**, some parodies, and some are about **silly topics** even if the background to the poem isn't **so silly**.

Bad hair: the cause of so much of my teen angst. Especially going to school in the morning when you're the kind of kid who chooses to sleep in until five minutes before the bus comes—leaving no time to do your hair. I figured I could have the best of both worlds and chop off my hair—keeping it manageable in the AM—and still have time to sleep while my sister was at the vanity. This didn't work out so well as my hairdresser and I realized that I am blessed with a head of hair that loves to stick up. This was just a little fantasy piece about finding someone who had hair that was crazy like mine, and who wouldn't mind having crazy hair with me. Awwwww.

The Cowlick

MORGAN C. McCORMACK

It's sticking way up in the air
One single little piece of hair
And now I know I look like hell
What's the solution? Must be gel!
It's wet and sticky on my hands
I look like I just joined a punk rock band
As I rub in all the Dippity-do
I hum the songs of Mötley Crue
I must hurry up to meet my fate
But he's now downstairs, I'm already late
And as I'm at the top of the stairs
All we can do is exchange wondrous stares
His hair is defying gravity as well
And all I can think is: "Ain't love swell?!"

This poem was spawned by a conversation about Archie Comics. My best friend and I were trying to figure out who our friends would be if we were in the Archies. I would be Betty, because I'm blonde and smart. Sarah, would be Betty, too. Sarah isn't blonde, but she's definitely not snobby and mean like Veronica. During this conversation we figured out that my first two boyfriends were Jughead. This was because they ate a lot, were goofy, and played the drums.

This poem was eventually set to music, and was recorded onto a tape that one of us has buried somewhere in our houses. We were going to have a band, and this was going to be one of our hits.

Note on the last line: I don't know why I chose to use a gun in the poem. I am a strong advocate for gun control and I have never even held a gun, I can't even stand to hold a toy one. I guess this is one of those examples for the disclaimer—"We do not support senseless acts of violence that may have been written about in a poem."

Jugheads

SARA BYNOE AND SARAH F.

One time Sara went out with a guy named James
Little did he realize behind his back she called him names
James's dream is to be like Conan—I guess that's why he works
    at A and W
James is a model and thinks that he can act
He'll pay for his trip to New York and then they'll send him back

James is a Jughead and no one likes a lazy boy
James thinks that everyone on earth will be his toy
What a Geek!

One time Sara went out with a guy names Cleetus
Cleetus is covered with zits
Cleetus thinks he's quite a catch—
I guess that's why Sara broke up with him at a pay phone
    at the mall
Cleetus is a drummer in all of Andy's bands
He's got warts on his face and you should see his hands
Cleetus is a Jughead just like James is, too
after one week Sara and Cleetus were through!
What a geek!

Sara can look back and laugh
because she never cared
and if she had a gun I bet the Jugheads would be scared.

This little ditty was conceived in a bus full of my softball teammates on the way to a tournament. It was also during the time of *Saturday Night Live*'s Deep Thoughts by Jack Handy.

Deep Thoughts
MICHELLE BJOLVERUD

Sometimes when I am riding in a van
I look at the window and I think it's raining
But then I realize it's just squished bugs

As a constantly despairing teenager, I was quite wordy with my woe. However, you wouldn't know it here. This is a great example of the silly bits that would get strung together in lieu of thinking too hard about how much pain I was in. (I know, I know.) And I didn't just write poems. I came up with titles for *collections* of my poetry. This list (which is, like, only a third of the original list of titles) is practically a piece on its own. A piece of what, I'm not sure . . .

"How to Kill Yourself Without Actually Dying"

"The Joy of Pain"

"Life and Other Weapons"

"Life and Other Punishments"

"Mirrors and Other Nasty Sources of Information"

"The Walking Wounded"

"The Story of the Wrong Girl"

"To Whom It May Concern, But Doesn't . . ."

"Five Feet Under"

"There's Nothing Good On"

Oy veh's mir!

I would sit on my bed and write. And write and write. I'm searching for that kind of discipline now! But at the time, it wasn't really discipline. It was necessity. It was like . . . breathing. Which I couldn't do unless I expressed some of the awfulness I incessantly seemed to be feeling.

I don't believe that this little ditty is about the boy that all my other poems are about. I think this is just me having fun with words. Also, get a load of the self-serving remark about sanity! Oh, I *must* be unbelievably crazy! Look at me, everyone, I'm nuts! It was so important for me to believe that I was off my rocker. I guess when you really *have* been feeling unstable for a significant amount of time, you start to get used to it. And God forbid someone should try to take that piece of your existence away from you. No wonder I was so sad for so long. I just couldn't let it go. It was how I defined myself.

You can still see the scars on my arms, but I no longer think of them as marks of defiance. They're symbols of strength. Sometimes other people notice them, too. I've had people suggest, "Cat scratches?," "Kitchen mishap?" Well, I'm allergic to cats. And if they're suggesting I got burned by a stove or something, I quote Carrie from *Sex and the City* when I say, "Cook? I use my oven for storage." No, these are my own (un)doing, and I'm glad they're there. They remind me of what I've overcome. How could I feel any other way?

Untitled

MELINDA GIDALY

You're the kind of person who—
when they were handing out brains
—took two.
I'm the kind of person where—
when they handed out sanity
—I wasn't there.

Other--Self-Appointed Themes

These poems just somehow do not fit into the other categories or the authors thought their poem did not **fit into the other categories**. These poems are about very specific situations of angst: moving, getting a **speeding ticket**, working for **minimum wage**, being goth, **being underage**, and lusting for **power**.

Part of the trauma of the teenage years has to be the drudgery and humiliation of fast-food jobs: being forced to wear ridiculous hats and put up with abusive customers, bullying supervisors, country music, and the pervasive smell of grease clinging to your hair, knapsack, jacket, etc., all for insultingly low wages. At least, that was my fast-food experience. And I didn't even get any fun out of my earnings, since I was just saving for university.

I didn't think I'd mind the job, when I first started. In fact, I was quite gleeful about doing drive-thru and being the voice from the box; plus, one of my best friends started working at the same place, which is probably the only reason I survived my year and a half there (before graduating to retail, which was much happier, though less conducive to bad poetry).

Anyway, I think I was working the dreaded 2–10 shift on a spring Saturday when I wrote this poem. I actually wrote it, very authentically, on a napkin.

Song of the Lonely Fryer Girl, or, Working in Fast Food on a Spring Day

JAN KRISTY

I'd sing for this sun, this blue sky
out the drive-thru window,
if I could
There is no sky in here
When the sun is gone
I'll still be at my post dying slowly
like this miracle day outside the window

Someone is falling in love on top of the Ferris wheel
I wish it was me
Someone is cutting their lawn just to enjoy the smell
Every day you live should be a jewel in your hair
not just dirt on your shoe
But what's one to do?
Someone is sailing a fine salt breeze
being dazzled by the brightness off the water
Someone is planting a row of marigolds
to keep the slugs out of their garden
Every day should be like that
golden flower
Not bludgeoned to death
for six dollars
an hour

This poem was the result of getting my second speeding ticket. I was a sobbing mess because getting another ticket meant my license would be taken away and at the time (I was sixteen) believe me, it was some seriously devastating news. I wasn't even driving my own car. It was my friend Joe's. He and I made a pact to marry each other if we both reach forty and are still alone ('cause forty is, like, SO old). He was so wonderful that night, simply driving around and not giving me any guilt trips about it being in his car. It was his gentlemanly behavior that inspired this verse—well, that and needing to get the "I hate cops" angst out. I remember thinking that I was being really cool just numbering my poems and not giving them any real titles, so the number eight really has nothing to do with anything besides my laziness.

#8

MORGAN C. McCORMACK

I'm sorry that your T-shirt got wet
From my own homemade rain
But your strong embrace,
Eased and aided my pain
Yelling at my window
I left my lava lamp on
I know instead of being there for me
You could have just gone
I wonder why you left with me
While others just shrugged
I wonder why you drove your car with me

Saying less than a bug
Please don't feel sorry for me
That's the last thing I want
Please don't beat up the others
Who make the choice to taunt
I'm a big girl
I can take care of myself
And for right now
The tears are on a big shelf
But they will come out
Perhaps a different way
Because I should save some up
For our wedding day

My family was moving houses during the time of high
school exams in grade eleven, and all the stress I had
came to a climax when all the books and other belong-
ings that used to sit in my room and comfort me with
their familiarity were packed away and moved to the new
house, yet I still had to spend one more night in the old. I was try-
ing to get to sleep on the floor (my bed, too, had already been sent
over to the new house), thinking over the joking conversation the
significant man in my life at the time and I had had that afternoon
(he had a funny way of pronouncing "mush" with a French accent),
and I just pulled out a piece of paper (I think it was the back of a
junk-mail flyer, the last things remaining in our house) and scribbled
down a poem in the half darkness. I keep it to remind myself of
that time, not at all a happy time. Exam results were bad, too.

A Stressful Time

TAMARA

Significant One: "How are you?"
Me: "Too many exams."
S.O.: "Falling apart. Becoming moush (mush)."
Me: "No, resting and rejuvenating so as to be better than ever."

Without free time, without free money,
Without much sleep, but with much pain.
Laugh on, you onlookers; it's funny
Me going quietly insane!
At school you'd called me strong; behold me.
I am a weakling in my heart.

Watch, as you had, so teasing, told me,
Your pride, your envy, "falling apart,
Becoming moush," as you had stated.
'Twas reflex spoke when I denied.
"No, resting, and being rejuvenated
For works ahead." Oh, how I lied!
It was true, kind of, then; not now.
I have no life, no night, no day.
I never had suspected how
Dependent I was on things of clay,
Material things that had surrounded
And carried me through hard times before.
Now they're a block away, but bounded
By walls and doors and locks and time
And time, and time, and time again, and more!
Come in my dreams; I need to rest.
Sleep? I wish, hoping for the best.
I sign yours truly, I remain
An erstwhile person, now not quite sane
Moush.

I wrote this in grade seven, after saying a stupid thing (in front of the gentleman significant to me at the time, of course!). It was among the first of the free-verse stream-of-consciousness poems I wrote when I was upset, and it is still the best one. I think people can relate to it most. We have all said things we wished a moment later we had never said. What was the mistake in my case? Don't ask me, I won't tell. As far as I know, no one else of the people who were in my class that day remembers it anymore. That is the way it should be. I read it over now, laughing at myself, but I know I still react in the same way on realizing I have said a stupid thing, though less dramatically and with more faith in people's bad memories.

A Mistake

TAMARA

Oh, why did I say that?
Ten thousand other things to say
Would have been perfect.
I could have
Just kept my big mouth shut.
But I just had to
Ruin everything.

My friends say:
"Don't worry."
"In ten minutes everything will be forgotten."
"You'll live."
"By tomorrow no one will remember."

Yet I know that they do remember.
Right now they are laughing behind my back.
Right now they are saying to everyone they meet:
"You know—ha-ha—what she said today?"
By tomorrow the whole world will know.

The guilt is burning inside me
Haunting me
Whatever I do, I cannot get rid of it.

If only I could turn back the clock
Or induce mass amnesia.
Anything's better than this,
Living with this shame.

I should kill myself.
Run away to the ends of the earth.
Take on a new name somewhere, say, in Indonesia.
Live as a hermit in the Andes.
(I know a nice high cliff I could jump off of
Straight into the water.)
It's better than this.

What should I do?
I still have to go to school tomorrow,
Face familiar faces,
And wonder: Do they remember?
Are they laughing and whispering and pointing
When my back is turned?
Or maybe they forgot.

But how should I know?

How do I know if they forget?
They know.
Some know far too much for their own good.

If only I could erase memories
Like pencil marks
Or cover them with Wite-out.

I would file this under the category "self-absorption/lust for power." This might be more of a male topic, but then what do I know about women? Perhaps it's a feeling of wanting to accomplish more in life than our fathers. Or maybe this could help explain why some teenage boyfriends are so in love with their girlfriend one day, and are complete a-holes the next day.

That feeling of "you're holding me back," is truly haunting. Is this what creates man-boys in their thirties? I don't know. There's just so much I don't know. . . .

"Never Get Tired"

G. MICHAEL GRAY
1997

I'm stuck in the middle
with mediocrity and hypocrisy.
Tonight I can be mistaken for arrogant
because I know I'm destined for greatness.

I want to leave this party before it ends,
because I refuse to be the tail.
Say what you want,
but I'm the one who never ends.
What I want will never die . . .
Admired forever . . .

This is a "lust for power"/"I'll show you" poem. This was written the first time I attempted to get into a nightclub. I was underage, but a friend and I dressed up like we were "college students." Instantly our cover was blown, our attempt at facial hair mocked, by an obese, out-of-shape bouncer, and with humiliation we were told to go home. I was furious, so I sat down on a nearby rock, pulled out my notepad, and wrote a poem about it.

"Electric Ave"

G. MICHAEL GRAY
1996

Bright lights blind you,
big stars steal the glory of the smaller ones.
Tiny pebbles get kicked farther,
and lesser people get used more.
Nothing's the way it ought to be,
love gets trampled every day.

Fat guys always become bouncers at clubs,
and skinny guys always get thrown out.
A terrier will nip at a golden retriever, and why?

For the taste of blood.
That's what we all want,
to take down something bigger than ourselves . . .

This is probably the worst "teenage trend" that I ever saw or participated in—people cutting themselves and carving up their own skin. I saw cut marks on a friend's arm, and ended up doing it myself. It wasn't deliberate copying, more like an idea that came out when I was feeling awful, and taking a shower, razor in hand, . . . it felt somehow, like a relief to feel hurt on the outside rather than the inside.

I started doing it privately, and hiding the marks from people, but I started noticing other eighth and ninth graders, always girls, with obviously self-inflicted wounds on themselves. It was obviously disturbing, and I started thinking of it as "the new anorexia or bulimia"—until one of my friends showed me how she'd carved the word PAIN in her abdomen. She had a cigarette burn on her inner arm, and decorated the surrounding skin with elaborate Sharpie-marker tattoos. That just crossed the line for me—this had become a sick fashion statement, especially with the group of goth-girl "Mansonites" (Marilyn Manson fans) that I knew. I understood the feelings behind it, but the sardonic poem was a reaction to how de rigueur it had become to display your fucked-upness.

Mutilate

SARAH F.
Grade 9, age 14

Look here everybody
I cut myself today
It's just so damn trendy
To display your rage and pain
Wear your inner anguish

Like a pair of ripped-up jeans
Ventilate your fury
Or else burst at the seams
I wonder if this turmoil
Ever settles in
The hurt is never real
Until it's on your skin

While I don't remember the particulars of "Kissing Vampires," I would bet good money that it was written soon after (a) reading *The Vampire Lestat*, or (b) listening to "Moon Over Bourbon Street" by Sting. Because it's spelled "Vampire" and not "Vampyre," I can date it to the high school years before my "Tragic Goth in black trenchcoat" phase.

Kissing Vampires

K. BANNERMAN

To kiss a vampire
Is to stab God
It's an icy plunge in blackness
It's a needle through the breast.

It's sleeping where the roots run deep
Twisting, gnarled, the roots are old and rotting.
It's a lust
It's like eating stars.

It's the theatrical encore
That hides in the shadows
Waiting for death to applaud.

How to Write Teen Angst Poetry

Step One: Experience a very intense emotion (anger, sorrow, hurt, loneliness, etc.).

Step Two: Make this emotion more intense by listening to angsty music.
Try grunge rock, Emo, punk, or girls with guitars.

Step Three: Get out pen and paper.

Step Four: Find a dark corner, light candles or incense—whatever you need to do to create a "mood."

Step Five: Let your heart pour out. Do not censor. It is a good idea to decide in advance if you want the poem to rhyme or for it to be more free verse, or you can just see what comes out.

Step Six: Write through the tears. The tear-stained pages are filled with the best teen angst poetry.

Step Seven: Keep writing until the emotion is purged from your soul.

Step Eight (final step): Do with the poem what you want. Hide it. Share it. Bury it. Burn it. I recommend keeping it and stumbling upon it in a few months so that you can have a good laugh at yourself.